THE 110%
SOLUTION

THE 110% SOLUTION

Mark H. McCormack

CHAPMANS
1990

Chapmans Publishers Ltd
141–143 Drury Lane
London WC2B 5TB

BRITISH LIBRARY CATALOGUING IN PUBLICATION DATA
McCormack, Mark H. (Mark Hume)
The 110% solution.
1. Personal success
I. Title
646.7

ISBN 1-85592-500-1

First published by Chapmans 1990

© Mark H. McCormack Enterprises 1990

The right of Mark H. McCormack to be
identified as the author of this work has been
asserted by him in accordance with the
Copyright, Designs and Patents Act 1988.

Photoset in Linotron Times by
Rowland Phototypesetting Ltd, Bury St Edmunds, Suffolk
Printed and bound in Great Britain by
Butler and Tanner Ltd, Frome and London

To my wife, Betsy, who has taught me the true meaning of 110% in every area of life.

I would like to acknowledge the immense help and assistance of Mark Reiter and Pat Ryan whose tireless efforts were invaluable in the preparation of this manuscript.

Contents

INTRODUCTION

The 110% Ideal

I have always admired athletes. It seems to me they embody an ideal that many of us strive for: giving life everything we have, applying ourselves 110%.

Watch Martina Navratilova storm the net and you see a purity of intention so extreme as to be awe-inspiring.

Watch Greg Norman set himself up to hit a drive, and the concentration is so intense it dazzles.

Watch Dennis Conner gybe a flying sailboat within inches of a buoy and the efficiency of effort is so well-honed you feel it in your solar plexus.

These people know what it means to give 110% – which is why they are champions.

It would be foolish to deny that they also are the beneficiaries of God-given skills and strength, attributes that set them apart from most of us. Still, there are plenty of fast, fit, well-coordinated women who are not Martina, and there are plenty of powerful men who are not Greg Norman or Dennis Conner.

Mere talent is not enough. Discipline, concentration and determination are the qualities that distinguish the great ones.

These qualities do not come easily and are not achieved by painless short cuts. That is the bad news.

The good news is that any of us can develop them if we have patience, desire and a capacity for realistic self-criticism.

1

In our personal ambitions, no less than on the playing field, the savvy to devise a strategy and the gumption to stick to it is of the essence.

But for all the analogies between the world of sport and what might be thought of as 'civilian life', there is one critical difference.

In the world of sport – certainly of professional sport – either you give it your all or you may as well stay at home. There is no alternative. In other aspects of life, however, there are millions of people who never break into a sweat, either literally or figuratively, and still manage to find a niche.

They can do this because there is no objective standard to which they must measure up. Their performance is gauged not in terms of batting averages or seconds on a timer's stopwatch, but in such vague language as 'Sally's doing pretty well', or 'Bob is getting a little careless'. And in civilian life it is easy to coast. If the Super Bowl Most Valued Player starts throwing interceptions, or if the Golfer of the Year begins shooting 75, it is immediately obvious he is slipping. If Joe Jones, the best lawyer or manager or account executive in Anywhere, USA, starts doing less than his best, the chances are that no one but a handful of his peers will notice. It might be decades before his reputation is spoiled. Of course, once it is spoiled, it is spoiled forever.

Still, in offices, in government bureaux, in our schools, people tend to discover that if they have any smarts at all they can slide by without putting out much more than a 50% effort.

Invest 75% and with a little luck you may even prosper. There is enough slack in day-to-day life to allow for that.

It has long been my conviction, however, that 50% or 75% simply isn't good enough. I'm not even talking about 'success' right now. I'm talking about happiness.

Having lived for sixty years, having run my own business for more than three decades, having dealt with people from around the world and in many different walks of life, this fact seems crystal-clear: Human beings feel their best when they are doing their best.

With peak effort comes peak self-esteem.

With peak concentration comes peak confidence.

With total involvement comes a sense of exaltation.

When you come right down to it, isn't that why we, as a culture, are so sports-crazy? We can flick on the television almost any hour of the day or night and see men or women trying their hardest. The spectacle is thrilling.

It is the premise of this book that this thrill does not have to be vicarious and it does not have to be occasional. All of us can experience the thrill of 110% effort ourselves. All of us can know the excitement and reward of holding nothing back.

It just takes practice, discipline, a certain amount of knowledge and a willingness to push beyond what you think of as your personal limits.

Let me address a fair question right now: Just who is Mark McCormack to be holding forth on the 110% solution to life? Can I claim with a straight face that I live up to this ideal myself?

Like the rest of us, I have lapses in attention, energy troughs, moments of preoccupation or fatigue when, try as I might, I simply cannot find within myself the stuff of top performance. Coming up short some of the time is part of what it means to be human. But that does not mean we should routinely accept less than optimal effort from ourselves.

We should be constantly aware of the differences between 50% and 75% and 110% effort. This 50–75–110% grid can be applied in almost any situation.

Let's say it is important for you to meet the chairman of your company.

The 50% solution is to think that it would be nice to run into the chairman in the lift.

The 75% solution is to figure out what you want to say to the chairman should you meet him in the lift.

The 110% solution is to plan your remarks *and* find out when the chairman uses the lift every day.

Can we turn our visions into realities? Will our ideas pass the test of practicality?

It is in this important area that I believe I can lay claim to a certain amount of expertise. You may want to fast-forward through the next few pages because they are a commercial (for me) – but it is a commercial with a point.

Some thirty years ago I left a secure and promising position with one of Ohio's leading law firms, Arter & Hadden. With $500 in capital, I launched a company designed to help golfers manage their business affairs. That was the seed from which our group of companies, the International Management Group, has grown.

I made my share of mistakes, but if I did one thing right, it was to think in international terms from the start. IMG anticipated the growth of sports around the world and realized that in order to service this growth and make our business viable we had to have a truly international presence.

As to the 'management' part of our corporate name, that too had to do with a fortunate hunch. It seemed to me that athletes were about to become major celebrities. There were three reasons for this: (1) the increasing amount of leisure time available to people in many parts of the world; (2) the astonishing impact of television, which brought the drama of sport into tens of millions of living rooms; and (3) the possibility that many companies would want to hire these new sports 'celebrities' as part of their overall marketing strategies. This, in turn, meant that professional athletes were going to need a lot of sophisticated help with their career planning and financial management.

Back in the middle 1960s nobody was truly representing sports personalities. There were a few people hustling the occasional investment deal, but to me the word 'management' meant a great deal more than that. It meant contract negotiations, tax planning, investments, insurance – the whole thing under one umbrella.

I believed passionately in the advantages of this approach. Fortunately, I was able to convince a good young golfer, Arnold

4

Palmer, of the advantages as well, and on a handshake he became my first client.

Next, it seemed only natural to build bridges with other promising players. The second and third golfers I signed were Jack Nicklaus and Gary Player.

A few years later we decided that if the concept worked with golf, why not tennis, a sport just then making the difficult transition into the big time of media legitimacy? We were fortunate enough to gain the confidence of Australia's Rod Laver and some years later signed sixteen-year-old Bjorn Borg. We represented the world's best racing driver, Jackie Stewart, and the world's best skier, Jean-Claude Killy.

IMG eventually mushroomed into a $1 billion business employing more than 1000 people and operating in 20 nations. I am proud to say we are still the industry leader in our original field – the representation of professional athletes – but that over the decades we have diversified. We represent the Nobel Foundation. We have participated in the commercial development of such classic events as Wimbledon, the British Open and the Kentucky Derby. Our television arm, Trans World International, has become the world's largest independent source and distributor of sports programming. Our classical music division represents such internationally prominent performers as Itzhak Perlman and Dame Kiri Te Kanawa.

Overall, then, the development of IMG is a happy story. But we also have had our setbacks and had to learn some hard lessons, and I am not ashamed to talk about them in these pages. After all, it is difficult to know what makes a good idea, unless you can identify what makes a bad idea!

I have seen promising executives reach a certain plateau of competence and responsibility, then stall. Why? Were they less bright or less fundamentally well-equipped than those who passed them? Not necessarily.

I have seen athletes with marvellous gifts fall woefully short of their potential, a tragedy that can't be measured just in monetary terms; what it really has to do with is the squandering of a life. Why does it happen? How can it be avoided?

What I have come to understand is that there are two kinds of mistakes: mistakes that come from trying too hard and mistakes that come from not trying hard enough.

Yes, you can err in the direction of too much effort improperly applied. Just ask anyone who has ever missed an easy return of service or been too aggressive in a negotiation.

But think about this. Mistakes that come from trying too hard are mistakes that you recover from. You even benefit from them because they teach you to wield your muscle with greater discretion. They are windows of discovery.

Mistakes that come from not trying hard enough are wasted opportunities, pure and simple. You learn nothing from them. All you walk away with is the sense of defeat and demoralization.

And perhaps the hardest thing to recover from is the habit – the disease, really – of just sliding by with the minimum of effort. This is the fatal error of believing that good enough is good enough.

It isn't.

I am a businessman. The emphasis in this book, as in my first book in 1984, *What They Don't Teach You at Harvard Business School*, is on careers and the workplace. That, after all, is where the bulk of my time is spent and where I usually observe my fellow humans. But I want to make it clear that business is just the lens through which I look at the world. It is not the entire world.

To put it another way, I don't want to narrow the scope of 'human behaviour' to mean 'business behaviour'. On the contrary, I intend to talk about business behaviour as it sheds light on how people function in general, what motivates them, how they get along, in all kinds of situations.

I want this book to be of use to the student who finds himself with three days left before finals and has to make a decision about how best to apportion his time.

I want this book to be helpful to the woman who is having her apartment painted and who must negotiate with the painters to give her the best job for the best price and with the least disruption to her home.

To be sure, I want this book to be of assistance to the executive trying to maximize the results of a business deal, but I *also* want to help him weigh whether the deal is worth cancelling a day off with his family. In short, I would like this book to help people establish priorities and keep their lives in balance.

I used to believe that success in business was about all the success you needed. If you built a good career, earned enough money, enjoyed a solid reputation in your field, you had made it and that was the end of the story.

Well, I don't feel that way any more.

I still believe wholeheartedly in the drama of business ambitions and in the rewards and gratifications of career success. Few things are as satisfying as the triumphant conclusion of a difficult piece of business.

However, I have increasingly felt the need to look at career ambitions and career triumphs in context.

Success in business, after all, is just one aspect of success in life, and it is success in life – comfort and confidence in dealing with others, enjoying a healthy self-esteem, knowing the joys of affection – that finally matters.

It is my sincere wish that this book will be of use to readers who take seriously that kind of all-embracing definition of success, and who are willing to devote 110% of their attention and energy to achieving it.

I also hope readers will understand that the 110% approach to life is *not* the only worthwhile approach. The world is a big place. It has room enough for people who put in their eight hours and bolt, room enough for those who daydream rather than perform. We cannot, finally, know the depth or quality of another person's experience, and we should never presume to think ourselves more inherently worthy just because we try harder. The goal is to be as demanding of ourselves as we choose to be, yet tolerant of others whose priorities are different.

CHAPTER ONE

First Things First

A great athlete cannot expect to make it to the top without a thorough grounding in the basics of his or her sport. Otherwise, there always will be someone more adept at the fundamentals (and hence more secure) who will be able to exploit the athlete's weaknesses – and push him or her back into the pack.

The same is true in business and in life. Before you can become a great salesperson, you have to make your first sale. Before the first sale, you have to decide if you like selling.

The following are basic to a 110% approach to life. You can build any type of success if you start with them.

1. Find your genius

Everyone, without exception, has a talent – something that comes easy to them.

It could be a talent for numbers, for working with children, for playing the trumpet, for getting along with people, for running a business, for lecturing, for swimming rather than tennis, whatever.

If you can find something you are really good at, you are more likely to succeed at it. You have given yourself a head start.

2. Don't deny your genius

The corollary to finding your talent, of course, is never denying what you are best at.

This is the sort of thing that is a dramatic staple of spy novels. The hero is a counterintelligence wizard who is fed up with spying and has retired from the business. Espionage is his genius, but he denies it. A crisis arises that only our hero can solve. His superiors beg him to come back. Whether the hero will use his talent or ignore it provides some manufactured tension, some bogus drama to the novel. In the end, we know, grumbling and complaining, he will come through.

While this sort of thing may be dramatic in fiction, in real life it strikes me as tragic – because it denies people one of the most gratifying experiences of life: the chance to live up to their potential.

Our client Bruce Lietzke is a genius at golf, an exceptional talent who could be one of the great ones. But he makes some peculiar decisions that, in effect, are a denial of his talent. He claims he doesn't like golf. He would rather go fishing, which is precisely what he did one year when the US Open was held in New York. Because he doesn't like New York, he skipped one of the most important tournaments of the year.

That is his prerogative. But as his managers, we don't find it dramatic or interesting, just frustrating.

The only thing worse than not finding your genius is finding it and wasting it.

3. Focus on today

Tomorrow will take care of itself. There's a lot to be said for having long-term goals, for having a vision of where you want to be in a month, a year or a decade, but not if it blinds you to the importance of what you are doing now.

I am much more impressed with people who can focus on problems that need immediate attention. They build their successes step by step, by concentrating on each new challenge as if it is the only thing that matters.

If there is an ideal example of focus, perhaps it is found in *Sports Illustrated*'s description of the great golfer, Ben Hogan, at the 1947 US Masters.

Hogan was paired with his friend, Claude Harmon, at the Augusta National's legendary twelfth hole, a simple-looking par 3 that is anything but simple to play.

Hitting first, Harmon lofted a beauty into the cup for the first Masters hole-in-one at the twelfth. The crowd roared. Hogan didn't say a word. He stepped up to the ball and hit it a few feet past the cup.

The roar intensified as the pair walked to the green. Harmon retrieved his ball, acknowledged the applause and stepped aside to watch Hogan study his putt and stroke it in for a birdie.

As the two men walked away from the site of Harmon's historic shot, Hogan finally said, 'You know, Claude, that's the first 2 I've ever made on that hole'.

That's focus.

Don't be distracted by what others do – unless you can use it to inspire you.

4. Trust candour

People have two options when they are in a jam. They can try to waffle around the problem, or they can open their souls and tell the truth.

Candour is the better option.

When in doubt, I am very upfront. If I have done something wrong, I admit it. If I am mad, I say so. If I am disappointed, I let people know. Candour is not only personally therapeutic, but it tends to calm most raw nerves. Sunshine, as they say, is the best disinfectant.

Candour can also set you apart from the crowd: most people are not as candid as they should be about what they have done or what they can do for you. Jean-Claude Killy once told me that an important reason he agreed to become our client in the late 1960s (when I was in my thirties and had virtually no presence in skiing or in Europe) was that I never promised him anything, whereas everyone else pursuing him was promising him the world.

Be candid with people in those moments when you have achieved far less than 110%. You'll find that they are more likely to remember your candour instead of your failings. They are also more likely to forgive you and to be equally candid with you.

5. Make your enthusiasm contagious

We've all known people who can 'light up a room'. They lift people's spirits with their energy, good humour and confidence simply by walking through the door.

A very successful money manager once told me about being photographed for a financial magazine at his home in the Bahamas. The photographer arrived with several cases of cameras and lighting equipment and proceeded to take over the investment guru's house and life for the day. He shot several different portraits of the man inside the house and in the garden.

The investment guru, by no means a timid soul, tried to protest. 'I'm a busy man,' he told the photographer. 'I don't have eight hours for pictures.'

Finally, with the sun setting in the background, the photographer announced that he had all the shots he needed.

When I asked the man why he tolerated such a massive intrusion on his time, he said, 'The fellow obviously had very high standards. He wasn't going to leave until he got the best possible shot. But what impressed me most was that he loved what he was doing. Who was I to interfere in the romance?'

Enthusiasm is catching. And when other people catch it, they will go out of their way to accommodate you, sometimes even when it inconveniences them.

12

6. Know your minimum requirements

The 110% ideal is not an absolute. It varies from person to person. To a professional golfer, a round of 80 may be disastrous but to a weekend hacker it may be a milestone achievement. An elite distance runner will not huff and puff through a seven-mile training run, but to the casual jogger the exercise may be a torture. All of us have our own definitions of peak performance.

Likewise, all of us have minimum requirements – how much time we need to do a job properly, how much rest we need to function at our best, how much food we need each day to avoid being grouchy, how much money we need to support ourselves and our family, how much social contact we need to feel stimulated, how much praise we need to stay motivated, how much exercise we need to feel good about ourselves.

The winners, in every walk of life, not only have a finely calibrated sense of their minimum requirements but they also have the discipline to resist distractions that tempt them to compromise on that minimum.

One of the toughest jobs in our business is telling a well-heeled sponsor that an athlete client is not available for his event. With the heap of money they put on the table, many sponsors simply cannot accept that a gifted athlete would rather rest or train or consult a coach, or spend time with family and friends, than work those additional days.

Kiri Te Kanawa, the great lyric soprano, is accomplished at calculating her limits and enforcing her minimum requirements. A beautiful voice is the most fragile gift, vulnerable to bad weather, colds, fatigue, arid hotel rooms and jet lag. Perhaps that is why opera singers are so temperamental and edgy. Yet Kiri is one of the most serene and confident people I know. She will go jogging in the park on the day of a performance.

Over the years she has figured out precisely how much time for travel, rest and preparation she needs to perform at her peak. And she doesn't waver from it.

'If you look at my pattern,' she says, 'it all really works if I get eight days between performances – three days before the

13

performance, two days after and then off to another engagement. I need those days to perform in the best vocal health. If I can't have that situation, I won't accept the job.

'To me, that's not opting out. If you can't do the job the right way, then look for work that you *can* do the right way. That's how I get my 110%. More often than not, I'm doing my job exactly the way I know I can be at my best.'

Even when concert promoters tempt her with outrageous fees to perform, she says, 'I go back to the main plan. I ask myself, "Given my physical limits, can I travel to the next city and sing well?" If I'm flying from London to New Zealand, I need ten days between performances. As a result, I have a tremendous amount of down time. I sing forty times a year. But I don't consider it down time. It is essential for the health of my voice.'

The net effect is that Kiri Te Kanawa rarely cancels engagements and remains in constant demand. As for her voice, her doctor says that it will be in even finer shape in her fifties. At an age when other singers are fading, she should be peaking.

By doing less, Kiri Te Kanawa is able to give more.

Calculate your minimum requirements. If you need eight hours of sleep to feel alert, don't try to get by on six. If you need four weeks to finish a proposal, don't say you will deliver it in two weeks. If you need to spend a certain amount of time with your family each day to feel connected and whole, don't settle for less.

Short-change yourself on what you need, and you will fall short on what you need to do.

7. Do what you love

The best thing about doing what you love is that it empowers you to keep going, to endure hardships and make sacrifices long after your competitors have quit for the day. That advantage is very hard for others to overcome. In fact, the hardships tend to become a satisfying part of the process.

David Frost, the television commentator, puts it this way: 'When you analyse the whole business of giving 110%, the key is getting great pleasure from the work. Though you are flogging yourself, you really gain stimulation and fulfilment.'

If you don't love what you are doing, you won't love succeeding at it. In fact, you probably won't succeed at all.

Billie Jean King on Achieving 110%

The secret of Billie Jean King's success in tennis is that she loves the game more than anyone I have ever known. She just gets a kick out of hitting tennis balls. I remember once at the Wightman Cup when my wife, Betsy Nagelsen, needed practice. She wanted to play with someone at 6 a.m. because she had to catch an eight o'clock plane. Billie Jean didn't hesitate. She said, 'I'd love to get up and hit with you.' And off they went to pound balls while everyone else was sleeping. That's Billie Jean. Besides the talent, the drive, the hard work and the incredible personality, she loves the game more than her opponents.

You have to go all out, you have to give 110% every day. If that intensity isn't there – whether it is in business or music or writing or sport – you can never experience the magic moments. They don't come often; they are the exceptions.

As a tennis player, I remember getting that feeling only three times: In 1974 at Forest Hills when I beat Evonne Goolagong in three sets in the final of the US Open. I came into that tournament really tired. Then winning at Wimbledon in 1975. Everyone had given up on me, and I knew it probably was the last time I could win there. And in 1976 when our team, the New York Sets, took the World Team Tennis Championship. That came after forty-three matches, plus the playoffs, and the high was even better because I got to share it with the men and women on the team.

Now, in business, the magic moments come in other ways. In 1985 I wanted to help local tennis by setting up a recreational team tennis league. We had six months to find a sponsor – and got one.

In a way athletes are spoiled. They set an objective and there is a score at the end of the day; they have won or lost. In business your assessment of whether you are succeeding or failing is subjective. Progress, whether it is in life or sport, is gradual. You have to back off, then go forward; but in the end you have to close the deal. You've done 99% of the job, but you still haven't got the signature or the first payment. That requires daily effort and persistence.

It's like being at match point, or two points from match point. You have to close. You must look forward to the toughest part. Champions relish the challenge; they must enjoy pressure and look on it as an opportunity, not a disaster.

In tennis, if you are in your winning mode, you are saying, 'OK, give me your best serve.' If you are in a losing mode, you are saying, 'Please, God, let her double fault.'

Champions wake up excited about the day. There is a commitment in your daily life. The intensity has to be there constantly. You don't have any waves or fluctuation in the intensity when playing or practising. It's all those days of giving 110% that equal the rare magic moments.

You need a schedule each day, certain goals to achieve. In business, it may be two and a half hours of phone calls, one meeting, two interviews. Every night or early in the morning, make a list. Write it down.

Some people expect instant gratification. They don't understand that they have to work, that there must be a daily ritual. That you have to learn your craft.

For each person winning is something different. Each of us has our own definition. In America we are taught from childhood winning is being No. 1, but that's not the case for everyone. Winning has to do with achieving your happiness. And that continually changes through the years. Winning for Jennifer Capriati at twenty will be far different than it is for her at fourteen.

When I'm teaching, all the players keep notebooks and write down their goals, before and after practice. They put down what they have learned. They must do this in their own voice, in their

16

own way, not in my words. Pupils have to become independent. They need high self-esteem. I want them to challenge me more and more. I should have less and less to say. And when I can't teach them any more, they should fire me quickly.

That's where Martina [Navratilova] is now. She has a full-time coach, Craig Kardon, and occasionally I come in for a jolt. Not being there every day can be helpful. We have Martina write down daily how she feels mentally, physically and emotionally. The mental aspect has to do with strategy and technique. Does she feel 80% or 100% physically? And emotionally, is she scared or happy? Or nervous?

You look for a pattern and you are able to evaluate your goals. I want Martina to decide what her goals are; they aren't what Billie Jean thinks they should be. I want her to decide what will make her a happy person.

The best way to get rid of painful things is to talk about them. Be honest about them. And once you express that verbally, you can get through it. But you must listen to yourself. Hear what you say.

Champions have a personality trait – they have a happiness and heartiness about life. I've known a few, but very few, that didn't. They know how to adjust, how to get through when things aren't perfect. They understand how to control their own destiny.

CHAPTER TWO

What Is Life Made of?

What is more valuable – something replaceable, or the rarity, that last bottle of a classic Burgundy, or a Van Gogh or a Bugatti? The answer is pretty obvious: the scarcer the object, the more valuable. Yet people put an absurdly low value on that truly irreplaceable commodity in their lives – time. It is just taken for granted, like air and water. But if the twentieth century has taught us anything, it is that no resource is inexhaustible.

There are only sixty seconds in a minute, twenty-four hours in a day, fifty-two weeks in a year – and just so many heartbeats in a lifetime.

Never mind that cliché about not having enough hours in the day. Forget what people say. Look at what they do. It becomes painfully clear that they do not cherish their time as much as they should – or use it effectively.

Whether the demands are mental or cardio-vascular (and I'm not persuaded there is much difference between the two), you have to gear up for top performance, and you have to stay geared up.

We all know the story about the fellow who goes to buy a used car, and the salesman tells him the previous owner was a little old lady who only drove to church and never exceeded the thirty-mile-an-hour speed limit.

Now, let's assume for a moment the salesman is telling the

truth. The fellow buys this cream-puff car, takes it out on the freeway and floors it. What happens? Chances are the car, which has never been driven fast, revs up to a neck-snapping thirty. The carburettor is full of sludge, the points are dirty and the plugs barely spark. A lifetime of low performance makes for a low-performance car. Much the same thing happens with people.

You can't expect to make low r.p.m. demands on yourself most of the time and then suddenly find the jolt of power needed to accomplish something you really want.

To make the best use of time, you have to make a habit of using it flat out – and well. Hard work is energizing and the more you push yourself, the more you can push yourself.

How Much Information Do You Really Need?

Ever notice how many commuters on the morning train spend the whole journey reading the newspaper? Now I'm not knocking newspapers, and I'm not quibbling with the responsibility of good citizens to keep themselves informed. I question, however, whether reading the paper is really the most useful thing these people could be doing at this particular time.

Most of us are mentally sharpest in the morning. Should that peak of alertness be used passively to absorb newsprint? Or put another way, to learn what everybody else is also finding out at that moment? We are told, over and over, that information is a powerful tool. True, but like every other commodity the value of information is subject to the law of supply and demand.

Information is worth less in proportion to how many people have it. If there is something only you know, the value of that information can be almost infinite. This is something always to remember when you are tempted to divulge a secret. But if you know what everybody knows – well, what's it worth?

Defensive Information

There are certain things a business person can't afford *not* to know. If you work on Wall Street, you obviously have to scan the financial pages. Given my business, I'd be foolish to leave myself vulnerable by not keeping abreast of goings-on in sport. But . . .

It is my conviction that a working professional should be able to extract what he or she needs from a newspaper in ten minutes.

For all the justifications that people come up with for spending their whole trip to work reading the paper, I think the real reason is that it is the path of least resistance; it is easier than anything else they could be doing.

They could be reading a book about their field; but reading a book entails a certain commitment. They could be working on the letters or memos they'll put off till later in the day – when, probably, their thinking won't be quite as clear. In short, they could be actively applying themselves to tasks that pertain to their careers and lives, rather than passively, automatically looking at the newspaper.

Why not save the paper for the evening ride when fatigue has rendered us unfit for more creative things?

Wait a Minute!

Every life and every job has its rhythms, whether you are the proprietor of a grocery or a house-bound mother with a toddler. There are stretches when you go flat out and others when you dawdle and dither.

If you aspire to lead a full life – to get 110% out of every day and not look back somewhere down the line at wasted opportunities – then my advice is to examine a typical week minutely. Do you mean to squander the time you do?

And while you have your pencil out, how about making a life list – what you want to have achieved or attempted before check-out time? Don't be hampered by your current status or the amount of money in your bank account. Do you want to learn to fly, or make an Amish quilt, or tour Tasmania, or own a racehorse?

There are moments when all of us do the equivalent of scanning the newspaper rather than create some news of our own. This could be time spent as a 'couch potato' in front of the television, when blessed silence would be more soothing or constructive. It could be a whole morning waiting for someone – for a friend to return a call, for a package to be delivered. Or minutes wasted standing in line at a bank or supermarket or restaurant.

Ask yourself whether better planning would cut back on those hours. They add up astonishingly. Remember, these are moments of *your* 'prime time' that you can never recapture. And you have only yourself to blame.

The 'I Don't Need to Rest' Syndrome

There is no denying that everyone's stamina has its limits. There are times when you must rest. Here is a cautionary tale about what can happen when someone fails to see the value of down time. A number of years ago, IMG hired an energetic woman as an account executive to scout the junior ranks in golf and tennis and line up future stars for IMG. She was particularly impressed by a West Coast junior and determined to bring the tennis player aboard as a client.

After putting in twelve-hour days at the New York office, she'd call him in California to check on his training. When he was competing in Europe, she'd manage to be there to root for him by piggy-backing these excursions on regular business trips. There were times when the executive went a week without sleep, dealing with the extra flights and backlog of paperwork that accumulated while she was tracking the player's progress.

The capper came at the French Open. The woman was not scheduled to be at the French, but she persuaded her boss that an appearance was crucial to maintain ties to the youngster. Her boss agreed to the trip, provided that certain pressing matters be wrapped up before she left. The upshot was that she went without sleep for several nights.

Then came the flight to Paris, the jet lag and the frenetic and wearing atmosphere of a major tournament. The bottom line is that our go-getter was running on empty. She had yet to learn . . . *You can be working hard and not working well. And vice versa.*

On the evening of her arrival there was a reception for players, press and invited guests. Our executive latched onto her protégé and, like the good host she was, asked if there was anyone he'd like to meet. Now this took place during the reign of Bjorn Borg, who happened to be both a client of ours and this teenager's idol. So she guided him across the room to where the Swedish champion was sipping a club soda and chatting with European tennis writers.

Catching Borg's eye, the account executive said, 'Bjorn, I'd like you to meet . . .'

And she forgot the junior player's name!

She was so exhausted, so overwrought, that her mind just went blank. Borg, a truly gracious fellow, handled the embarrassing situation as well as it could be handled. But the kid was crushed. He flushed, stammered – and would never again believe in the sincerity of our executive's interest in him.

The irony, of course, is that her interest was sincere. But a gaffe like that, even though the cause was simple fatigue, is terribly destructive. The player went on to be ranked in the top ten in the world and never did become a client of our company.

But, as I have said, mistakes that come from trying too hard are ones you recover from – this hard-working lady has had a fine career with us.

The Executive Nap

I am a believer in the efficacy of the one-hour snooze – or even the fifteen-minute period of relaxation where you simply lie back, close your eyes and let your mind empty.

Some people call this meditation. I call it survival. Most people have an energy trough after lunch. If you've been up (as I often am) since 5 a.m. and have a business and/or social engagement in the evening, you gain more than you lose by dropping out for an hour in what is usually a relatively flat part of the day.

I realize that most working people do not have the luxury of taking siestas. And I'm not suggesting that corporate America shut down every business day between two and three.

Often the best way to emerge from an energy trough is not to fight it. That way, you won't lose even more precious energy. Simply give in and relax.

So don't panic, and don't berate yourself. Close your eyes, if only for one minute. Splash cold water on your face. Rev up gradually, and you'll find that your restored energies will carry you through the rest of the day.

Lying Down on the Job

On second thoughts, why couldn't America have some form of institutionalized siesta? Other countries do.

One of our executives was recently in China, meeting with one of the world's largest silk manufacturers. In the past, this company exported only raw textiles. Now it was eager to sell finished garments.

It was contemplating a line of sportswear, promoted by an IMG client. The travel arrangements to Beijing were, by Western standards, rather loose, so our executive was told simply to come by whenever he arrived; the chairman would make himself available all day.

Our executive showed up at 1.30 p.m. The compound was enormous – huge brick buildings spreading in every direction – yet the place seemed strangely devoid of noise and bustle.

Our executive soon realized why as his driver escorted him inside. The first thing he saw was a receptionist stretched out on a mat on the floor, fast asleep!

'Ah,' said the driver. 'Sleep time.'

23

The driver then led our executive, almost on tiptoe, down a corridor that branched into offices, design rooms and tea lounges, where open doors revealed dozens of sleeping workers peacefully stretched out on the floor.

Finally our executive reached the chairman's office – a large suite of spartan design. At a plain desk sat the chairman's personal assistant, with his head on the ink blotter, contentedly snoring. And through the half-opened door to the inner office, he saw the chairman sacked out on a sofa with a handkerchief over his eyes.

'You wait here,' the driver whispered. 'Sleep time almost over.'

Our executive sat down in a silk-upholstered chair. Within minutes, amid the soothing atmosphere, he too drifted off to sleep.

Precisely at two o'clock, a bell rang and women started scurrying around, distributing cups of tea. Three minutes later, the chairman had shown our executive into his office and was chatting away as brightly and cogently as if it were 9 a.m. on a spring morning. After his nap, he was ready to go 110%.

The two men concluded their business and the chairman provided a tour of the facilities.

'I have never seen a workplace so bustling,' our executive later told me. 'Everyone was on his toes, everyone was concentrating.'

A Western-style efficiency expert might bemoan all the worker-hours lost at nap-time. But given the visible results, I have to believe that the rest period was a very sound investment in human capital.

Efficiency: Knowing When Enough Is Enough

One of the most efficient people I know is a freelance copywriter who has done a lot of work for our firm through the years. I have never known him to miss a deadline or fail to keep an appointment. I have never seen him obviously overburdened, though I know he juggles half a dozen projects at a time. By his own admission, he is seldom out of bed, let alone on the job, before 9 a.m. He makes a quite adequate, if not princely, living, maintains his professional contacts and has kept his career moving upward while almost never working more than four hours a day. Clearly, this man knows how to maximize the returns on his time.

Other people plod through sixty or seventy hours of work a week. That isn't always necessary. Michelangelo, it is said, carved marble faster than an ordinary stonemason – so much for the romantic myth that creative work must be tormented and slow.

You need to learn when a job is finished. That is a skill which a surprising number of people lack; they keep nattering over a project long after the time for any meaningful refinement or improvement has passed. If you can improve 2% on what you have done but it takes two days or two weeks to achieve that, forget the extra effort. Your customer will not detect – or value – a 2% improvement.

Jean-Claude Killy on Achieving 110%

Jean-Claude Killy is the epitome of a champion – dashing, handsome, accomplished. His three gold medals in skiing at the 1968 Grenoble Winter Olympics made him a national hero in France.

Killy always had a daredevil streak on the slopes, but it was backed by a tremendous confidence and inner steel. I got a glimpse of this our first dinner together in 1967. He ordered a glass of wine and I made a crack about how he was breaking training. He sipped from his glass and said, 'Would you rather I drink milk and skied like an American?'

Unlike many athletes, who don't have the patience for a second career in business, Killy has become celebrated again by bringing the 1992 Winter Games to Albertville, France. Selling your city as the Olympic host can be a politically tricky, even ugly, business. But as co-president of the 1992 Organizing Committee Killy succeeded with panache.

*He approaches business the same way he attacked the slopes –
with 110% energy and efficiency. Jean-Claude is simply willing
to outwork everyone else.*

I think it is not a matter of *doing* 110% better so much as *being*
110% better than anyone else. Your whole person has to operate
at 110%. What is necessary is something that permeates you;
this something cannot just be whipped up when the moment
calls for it.

If you want to be the best skier in the world, it really is a
question of how you can ski faster than the maximum one thinks
is possible, *regularly*, at a comfortable pace.

When I won the triple gold at the Olympics, I was looking for
hundredths of a second. I won the downhill by .08 of a second,
which wasn't much, but to do it I had had to become comfortable
at a pace no one else was used to.

You must be very pragmatic. There are four steps you can
apply to any problem or area where you want to succeed: analyse
the problem, look ahead, decide, execute. You must be able to
do each of these at 110% in order to carry out the plan, to be
the 110% person.

It is important to realize that you can modify things. *Never*
accepting things as they are is very important. To invent where
there is nothing to invent: that is leadership.

Because I performed in a world where time was critical, I am
passionate about efficiency. I believe in exploiting it in order to
gain free time. This translates into every detail of my life, even
the way I pack my bag. All of my shirts go with all of my jackets,
which go with all of my trousers. I always have to be ready to
move quickly and look elegant. I ask for the same seat on the
airplane, close to the door so I can be the first one out and the
first one to grab a taxi. Maybe it just means I get to bed earlier,
get fifteen minutes more sleep.

I have so much to discover, to explore, and I cannot bear to
waste time. I like to maximize it. A system is very critical. I am
certain this attitude springs from my family roots, which are
Swiss, German and Alsatian. And to an overwhelming sense

that I have had since my youth that time is finite. I never wanted to lie on beaches when I was young because I always had this sense of urgency, this feeling that it could all end tomorrow.

The loss of my wife, Danièle, who died of cancer in 1987, sharpened this sense. It was a turning-point. My whole system of life crumbled and I had to put everything in order again. I analysed this tragedy and saw that it had provoked a complete change in the way I look at the world. While my work is important in terms of my personal development, I am a much more detached businessman. There is a phrase in English, 'gentleman farmer'; well, I am a gentleman businessman.

I sense the end coming. I don't hold so tightly to the things of this earth. I have had a chance to meet people who are exceptional – I don't mean movie stars, people who are famous or on magazine covers this week, but ones who do things in a manner unlike others. They refuse the conventional established order. People who find solutions far different from the usual ones. These encounters are what interest me now.

Facing up to the Hard Part

It isn't only what you do, or even how you do it – but also when you do it.

The notion that one should do things in a logical order is as old as the hills. Or at least as the Book of Ecclesiastes: 'To every thing there is a season, and a time to every purpose under the heaven. A time to be born, and a time to die; a time to plant, and a time to pluck up . . .'

The challenge that remains ever-fresh is to decide every day the logical order for a different set of tasks.

Let's say I come to the office one fine Thursday morning and I've got the following tasks ahead of me:

- a stack of internal memos to read
- a batch of external mail to go through
- a call to a long-standing client who has a problem

27

- a call to a much newer client who needs reassurance
- a call to a major advertiser who is thinking of pulling out of sponsorship of one of our events
- a speech to prepare for a presentation that evening.

The *real* first job of the morning – and the one that should keep you most alert – is to put all the jobs in order. Every day should be different. As soon as you fall into a rigid, habitual pattern, you are no longer operating at peak efficiency.

Things have to be measured one against the other as they happen. Many people in business – perhaps the majority – skip this first step and fall into a routine that they blindly follow, day in, day out.

Some work the telephone first. Some always do the mail first. These patterns then become habits which demand no conscious thought or serious decision-making. Sometimes, that can pass for efficiency. But I would argue that this 'automatic pilot' approach to structuring time is unresponsive to actual events and therefore not efficient at all.

Ninety-nine per cent of the time, you're best off if you attend first to the task you dread.

Let's say you've got five things to do. One you actually look forward to. Three you're pretty neutral about. The final one makes your blood run cold.

Nothing would be more natural than to tend to the pleasurable obligation first and to put off the one that concerns you as long as possible.

Don't do it!

A dreaded chore is the functional equivalent of a bad belly-ache. It poisons your mood. It clouds your mind. It preoccupies you and it lessens your effectiveness at everything else you may be called upon to do. So meet it head-on and get it over with.

I remember, a number of years ago, having an early breakfast meeting with one of our executives. He had a task in front of him that no one would have envied: to tell one of his long-standing clients – an associate and also a friend of fifteen years

28

– that his most visible and lucrative endorsement contract was not being renewed.

Over breakfast, the executive and I discussed the probable impact of this news. The client in question was a great athlete who had been retired for some years. He had made a lot of money during his playing days and had managed it prudently. The cancellation of the endorsement would not really hurt economically – even though it would cut his income by something approaching a million dollars a year.

No, the problem wasn't money; it was pride. The end of the highly visible advertising would be a painful reminder that this man's moment had passed. To someone still young – by standards other than those of professional sports – this would be hard to take. Add to that the fact that the client and executive fished together and shared family outings.

I pepped up my executive as well as I could over breakfast, and I assumed he'd make the difficult phone call at 9 a.m. I ran into him in the hall around 10.30 and he looked awful. I didn't even have to ask him if he'd made contact – I knew he hadn't just from the forced way he talked about other things.

I saw him again after lunch and he was positively ashen. I hoped he didn't have anything else delicate to handle that day because he couldn't possibly have done it well. His whole day, in fact, had become an unproductive holding action against the one thing he really had to do.

He finally came into my office around 6.30 that evening – and he was all smiles. He looked like a different man. He'd finally called the client, and the client had taken the bad news better than we'd expected. This was a world-class competitor, after all, a guy who'd learned long ago that you can't survive by betting your dignity and your self-esteem on the next small battle you win or lose.

'You know what he told me?' my colleague said. 'He'd had a better run than anyone had a right to expect. Now that part of things was winding down, he wanted to spend more time on community projects, unpaid things where he could give something back. He actually sounded happy about it. Jeez, why didn't I call him earlier?'

I fought the temptation to say, 'Well, why *didn't* you?' I figured the executive had learned a lesson without my rubbing it in.

Imagine if that call had been made first thing in the morning. The relief that came from a tough task completed would then have powered him through many productive hours. It would have put him in an upbeat mood. It would have set him up to apply himself 110% to the day's remaining jobs – which would have seemed easy by comparison.

Don't limit this advice just to business dealings. How many times have you heard a friend, or someone in your family, or indeed yourself, fret and talk endlessly with anyone who will listen about conveying some bad news? The hours spent agonizing over what to say seem to grow in proportion to the pain of the problem. Some people talk all around it, ruining whole weeks of their lives, and never, in the end, face up to the dreaded deed. The consequences can be devastating.

Make Time to Think About Time

I once heard a harried executive exclaim, 'I don't have time to worry about time management.' I'm not sure if he was bragging or being ironic, but the statement certainly said a lot about why he looked so harried.

This fellow was breaking the first rule of getting organized.

1. You must take some time to take control of your time

I spend at least an hour of each business day thinking about how I can get the most out of the remaining twenty-three hours. On paper this doesn't sound particularly difficult to do. Most people believe they already are doing this.

But when was the last time you made a 'to do' list *and* allocated a specific amount of time to get each task done? More to the point, when was the last time you listed 'time management' at the top of your list? If you're just listing tasks *and not estimating the time they take*, you have a lot more planning to do.

2. Time is money

Most people know the phrase. But not enough put it into practice. For example, at this point in my life, I could legitimately be spending all of my time in any of a half dozen cities where our company does business. As a result, I have been forced to become very disciplined about my schedule. Nearly every decision is a risk-reward calculation filtered through the clock.

If I visit our Toronto office, will the resulting business for our company represent fair compensation for how I value each hour of my time? If that is worth, say, $500 an hour, will the thirty-six hours I spend in Toronto return $18,000 to the company? That is what I mean by time is money. I'm not sure if most business people interpret the phrase in quite the same way.

When was the last time you assigned a financial value to an hour of your time? When was the last time you flew from New York to Los Angeles and (together with the cost of the round-trip ticket) considered the true cost of those hours on the road? If you were kept waiting two hours for a doctor's appointment, would you bill the doctor for your time? Hardly, but maybe you should consider changing doctors.

3. Make each minute count

A lawyer in our New York office pointed out to me that she has never met with me at the top of the hour. I am always scheduling her appointments at oddball hours such as 9.25 or 11.10.

I don't do that on purpose all the time, but I think people waste time by rounding off the clock and scheduling activities on the hour or half-hour. Life is more haphazard than that. Not every meeting ends on the dot. What are you doing with all those extra minutes before your 10 a.m. or 3.30 p.m. appointment?

In my experience people pay more attention when you are

very specific about time, and the best way to be specific is to pick an odd time. If I tell someone I'll pick them up at their hotel at 12.08, even if I'm half joking, that somehow grabs their attention more vividly than saying I'll pick them up at twelve o'clock or 'around noon'.

Precision with time not only saves you time but forces the other side to be at least as precise as you are.

This technique is just as valuable outside the business world where, for some reason, people tend to be even more cavalier with your time. Neighbours would never dream of stopping by your office 'sometime in the afternoon'. Yet they become incredibly imprecise and relaxed about time when it comes to stopping by your *home*. They'll make a date for 1 p.m. and show up forty-five minutes late without calling. They'll promise to visit and cancel at the last minute. You'll invite them over for a quick chat and they linger for hours.

Fixing a precise or odd time in someone's head lets them know you ration your minutes.

CHAPTER THREE

The Tango of Time

We assume that each of us controls the use of our time. It isn't that simple. How well we use it depends, to a large extent, on how successful we are at persuading others to let us use our time to maximum advantage. We have to prevent others from wasting our time. This calls for alertness, assertiveness and tact.

Time is something of a tango. To dance the tango well, you've got to know how to move gracefully with others, when to follow, when to lead – and when to change partners and move on.

People can be reasoned with. They can be motivated and given incentives. They don't like to be rushed, but usually they are sensitive to other people's deadlines, goals and rhythms. Don't count on it, however. Never assume that someone else will use your time efficiently.

It is *your* time, after all, and you have to take the lead in making sure it isn't squandered. How does one do this?

Always have a clear idea of how long a given conversation, meeting or negotiation should take.

This does not mean that one should approach things with the rigid mentality of an egg-timer. What it does mean is that one should think through in advance the substance and complexity of a given matter, and allot it neither more nor less time than it deserves.

From traffic jams to snowstorms to air traffic delays, there are all sorts of natural and unnatural impediments waiting to snarl up your day. There are plenty of things one simply can't control. Which makes it all the more important to stay on top of things you can control.

Take your schedule, for example. You should always try to schedule the end of a meeting at the same time as you schedule the beginning.

This is common sense, yet hardly anybody seems to do it. Everybody agrees that it is crucial to get to the next appointment on time. How can you do that if you leave the ending of your *last* appointment to chance?

Let's say I'm arranging to call on an executive of a company that sponsors one of our golf events. At the time of scheduling the meeting, I'll say something like this: 'Two o'clock, Bob? That sounds fine. But I have something at three, which will take me around twenty minutes to get to. Does that leave us enough time – or shall I try to do some rearranging?'

Now, think about the different things this simple statement accomplishes. Obviously, it sets a time for the meeting, but that's the barest minimum.

It also sketches out the duration – i.e., forty minutes. However, it does so in a flexible way. What I'm not saying – and this is very important – is, 'I can give you only forty minutes of my precious time.' That approach is arrogant and abrasive, and anyone who uses it is heading for a fall.

What I am saying is, 'Let me know now if you need more time.' Putting it this way has advantages: it encourages Bob to organize his thoughts and so increases our chance of having a focused and productive *tête-à-tête*.

If Bob does say he needs more time, this gives me a valuable tip-off that he has something consequential to discuss and so allows me to prepare accordingly. And it spares me the potential awkwardness of having to announce out of the blue, at 2.35, that I have to leave in five minutes.

Finally, setting up the appointment in this way makes Bob feel good. I'm letting him know that our time together is important enough to me that I don't want to let it be short-changed. Note that I'm not promising I can rearrange things to suit him – maybe I'd be able to, maybe it would simply be impossible. But I'm making a sincere offer to accommodate his needs.

Don't Be a Facts Machine

In a misguided attempt to be efficient, some people never bring a conversation around to a human level. In fact, they don't have *conversations* at all; what they have are 'data-swaps'. They spit out facts, in return for which they pump you for information.

People like this imagine they are being businesslike. They think they are saving time by never asking how your kids are, how your summer is going, how you fared on your last fishing trip or member-guest golf tournament?

This is a very false economy in terms of time. Maybe these omissions save you a few hours here and there. But you lose the opportunity to become a real human being in that person's eyes. You lose the opportunity to move from being someone that person might do business with to someone that person would *choose* to do business with.

Avoiding Phone Tag

I would like a penny for every minute wasted in the world on Phone Tag – every time you call someone who is: (1) out of the office; (2) in a meeting; (3) in the bathroom down the hall; or (4) 'around here somewhere, but I can't find him'. And every time he calls you back, *you're* unreachable! Within a year, I'm sure, I'd be rich as the Queen of England.

Phone Tag can't be eliminated altogether. We're not chained to our desks. Still, there are a couple of extremely simple ways to ensure that the game doesn't go on for ever:

1. When speaking to someone's secretary or assistant (or

35

their wife or room-mate), you should always ask for a specific time that person can be reached.

2. When leaving a message on an answering machine or with a receptionist, leave a time or times when you can be reached. If you can't be reached, give the other party the courtesy of letting him know.

The Race

The effective use of time is a cooperative enterprise.

This is so even when the use of time appears to be *not* cooperative but competitive. Consider the most apparently time-competitive situation of all: a foot-race.

In a foot-race, for anyone to run supremely fast, something that looks suspiciously like teamwork has to take place. Someone has to set a fast pace early on – a remarkably selfless task since, except in sprints, the runner who breaks first from the blocks almost never wins. Someone has to go stride-for-stride with the eventual champion during the gruelling middle of the race. Finally, someone has to push the winner through his or her finishing kick, pressuring the victor to reach back for that final bit of strength and will.

When you take a world-class runner and stick him in a mediocre field, you rarely come away with a memorable performance.

The dynamics of a race have useful analogies in the day-to-day functioning of organizations. Some companies establish a sluggish pace right from the start. Whether from the top down or the bottom up, they create an atmosphere in which course records are unlikely to be set. Other companies, by contrast, don't just provide a fast track – they *are* a fast track. Time-efficiency is stressed across the board. Extra effort, far from being reserved for special occasions, is the order of the day.

Let's say I call my secretary in and give her a stack of documents to be Xeroxed. Now if, when she arrives, I'm leaning back in my chair with my feet on the desk, playing with Rubik's cube, the chances are that she'll take the documents, plop them on *her* desk and leave them there while she has a cup of coffee and makes a couple of personal phone calls.

Why should she do otherwise? If I'm slacking, why shouldn't she? If, in the boss-secretary tango, I'm setting a languorous pace, it's only natural that she'll fall into step.

But let's say she strolls into my office for the Xeroxes, and I'm already drafting the next memo. In that case, she'll go at a very different clip. She knows there is more work to follow and no time for a backlog. I'll actually see the change in her step – it will be springier, more resolved. She'll practically jog to the copying room.

Yes, there's an element of competition involved – but it's a comradely competition, and it's directed towards a common purpose. At the end of the day, I can look at a significant amount of work that has been done and can honestly say to my secretary, '*We* did a good job today.' And I can truly believe that my secretary made *me* more efficient, just as I made *her* more efficient.

This sort of dynamic happens all the time in all walks of life. It is surely one reason people yawn at the same time or cross their legs the moment someone else does. Consciously or not, people tend to be mimics or chameleons. They have an uncanny knack for gauging the pace and rhythm of their counterparts and then matching it.

I see this (and often use it to my advantage) in business. Sometimes in a meeting, my speech pattern is consciously abrupt and clipped. My comments are brief, suggesting I am in a hurry. If I do this consistently, the chances are that the other people in the room will pick up my pacing cues and assume an equally brisk manner.

Conversely, if I present my case slowly in long, carefully measured statements, the other side is more likely to be extra thoughtful in its response. If I talk softly, they are less likely to be bombastic.

Another Time to Slow Down

Slow decisions are usually better than fast ones and no decisions are better than wrong ones. And yet the world prefers fast decisions to slow ones, wrong ones to none at all.

If you detect a conflict here, you're right. In an accelerated age, where people put a premium on speed and hyper-efficiency, effective decision-making seems to be in direct conflict with how we like to use our time.

Almost any decision that can be slowed down should be slowed down. Fight like mad against the impulse to rush a decision.

Unfortunately, a lot of people can't deal with that. They're impatient. They can't wait. For whatever reason, they need a decision now. And so they importune us for snap decisions. They make us supply answers as quickly as they ask questions. And that is a dangerous way to work.

A key to making slower decisions is to accept that, quite often, nothing bad will happen if you can't or don't decide.

Doctors (and the nurses who handle their appointments) are masters at this. If you call your doctor with an urgent complaint, what happens? The chances are that you don't even get through to the doctor. You talk to the doctor's nurse, who asks a few pertinent questions and then informs you that the earliest date the doctor can see you is two weeks from Monday.

'Should I schedule you for the morning or afternoon?' asks the nurse, calmly throwing the decision back to you.

The nurse, in effect, is asking you: How serious is this? Serious enough so that you are willing to make a nuisance of yourself and demand to see the doctor right away? Or can you wait two weeks, by which time the pain may have gone?

Doctors know that most patients' complaints don't require immediate attention, so they have become masters at deferring or delaying decisions until more information is available – in this case, until two weeks later when you may be feeling much better.

It's a great system. It lets doctors address problems at their pace rather than the pace of their patients. And it works in the majority of cases.

The same thing happens in the business world. Ray Cave, who was the managing editor of *Time* magazine for eight years, once told me he simply refused to decide half the problems his staff presented each week. That's not because Ray is indecisive. As managing editor, he had one of the most decision-intensive jobs in America. He faced scores of queries daily. And these weren't small, self-contained choices on the order of whom to phone, whose calls to return or where to have lunch. Ray's decisions had a direct impact on dozens of talented people around the world.

If he opted to run one story rather than another, that set off a chain of consequences for a battery of reporters, writers, editors and photographers. It also lit a fuse on a string of other decisions. Once Ray knew what story was going in the magazine, he also had to decide who would write it, how long it should be, what pictures to use and who should take them. And so on, for every page of the magazine while the clock insistently ticked away towards the weekly Saturday deadline and more and more people streamed into his office, urging him to make even more decisions.

Eventually, to preserve his judgement, sanity and budget, he learned to make non-decisions. And not surprisingly, given that circumstances and news events around the world change by the hour, nearly all of the so-called pressing problems went away or popped up again in different guises. Either way, any decision would have been moot.

As Ray explains it, 'If people were urging me to assign a story and I wasn't sure it was a good idea, I'd sit on it. I'd rather lose a day of reporting than have someone start on the wrong story and then have to stop and start on something else.'

Another key to making slower decisions is figuring out why other people want you to go faster.

The classic example of this is the salesperson with a quota. Salespeople always make more sales near the end of their monthly or quarterly sales cycle because they employ tactics to speed up the customer's decision, such as lower prices, added incentives and inventory clearances. In most cases, a shrewd customer would be better off deciding even more slowly – to make the salesperson more desperate and improve the terms.

Most of us can sense when people are pressing us for a quick decision. But sometimes the process is very subtle; the hidden agendas are hard to detect.

For example, one of our executives is a whizz at public relations and handling the press. Nothing delights him more than arranging a television or newspaper feature that promotes me.

I've never liked doing interviews and don't have much time for them. Yet he is constantly urging me to schedule these interviews, sometimes months in advance and well before I really want to lock up certain parts of my calendar. He says they promote our company and our clients. He makes it sound as if he's doing me a great favour.

It took me a while to realize that I was doing him the favour. Lining up interviews was making him look good with his press contacts. The faster I decided, the more effective he appeared. In a way, he was scoring points with the press at the expense of my schedule. Once I figured this out, I didn't feel as bad about putting him off for a couple of months or telling him no.

In recent years, a third element has appeared to hasten the decision-making process: high technology.

Word processors smother us with documents, seducing us into believing that we are adequately informed.

Fax machines make even the most trivial request seem urgent.

Overnight deliveries force us to respond in kind. We make decisions overnight.

Not long ago I was reading a history of George Washington's dealings with his generals during the French and Indian Wars. It would take weeks or months for news of a devastating massacre of settlers to reach Washington from the frontier. Washington would rage, thump his desk and demand immediate vengeance. He would fire off orders – demanding that reinforcements be mustered immediately and deployed West.

But given the methods of communication and transportation in the 1780s, his commands moved at a pony's pace. It would take months before the men could be gathered, kitted out and trained. By then, Washington's anger would have cooled, the emergency wasn't an emergency any more and the nation's slim resources could be used for something more rewarding.

All of which makes me wonder whether the new office technology is not prodding us too quickly to make decisions that need far more thought.

Evonne Goolagong on 110% Timing

Evonne Goolagong is one of the least complicated athletes I know. Her signature on the tennis court was a gliding, effortless style. She made winning Wimbledon at the age of nineteen look easy. She also made the transition from champion athlete to motherhood look easy, which of course it wasn't. In 1980 she became the first and only mother in the modern era to win a Wimbledon singles title. Great female athletes usually defer having children until their playing days are over. But in Evonne's case, motherhood made her more disciplined about time and more focused. She now lives in Naples, Florida, with her husband, Roger Cawley, and their two children.

With fishing, I forget everything. It's nice to be out in the sun. Peaceful. And there's so much to learn – about the tides and my little tackle box and all those coloured lures. When I catch fish, I scale them, gut them, cook them. It's satisfying.

I loved tennis in another way. It was my business. I had a fluid way of playing. The first year I competed in England, I remember some Australians watching me. 'We came to watch because you're so graceful,' they said. That was a shock, something I had never realized. Later people would ask me, 'Have you ever taken ballet lessons? You make it look so easy.'

But I was trying my guts out. Some people thought I didn't even care.

I liked to get into a rhythm and knew that if somebody complained about calls and broke up the play, it was breaking my rhythm. I was never the type who blew up – that embarrassed

41

me. When Chris Evert and I met, there never were going to be arguments. Chris and I could have gone through our championship matches without an umpire or linesmen. We would have told each other whether the ball was out. That's what I liked. Getting on with the game.

The one person who put a lot of pressure on me was Billie Jean King. She seemed larger than life because of the aggressive way she presented herself on the court. It used to put me off; I spent more time watching her than concentrating on what I was doing. She'd start arguing with the umpire and then everything became so dramatic.

One of my most exciting matches was in the US Open in 1974. Billie Jean beat me in the final, three sets, 7–5 in the third. We were playing out of our minds. We had this unbelievable rally where I thought the point had ended several times, but it didn't because both of us were just throwing each other around the court. And suddenly it finished. I remember, my hair stood up on my arms. It was just so exciting even though I lost.

You have to show confidence on the court. I sensed Chris could feel when I was playing well. She'd peer over at me to see how I was reacting. There are times I feel confident even before I get on the court.

In 1980, when I won at Wimbledon, I couldn't wait for play to start. I was just so excited the whole tournament. I felt as if I was blessed during those two weeks.

I had had my daughter Kelly in 1977 and after that I came back in four months. I had a Caesarean section and I was so weak. I thought the ball was going to knock me over. The first tournament I played in – six months after her birth – I went out in the first round. It just about killed me. I went back to the hotel and slept for twelve hours. And I said, uh-oh. I guess I'm not ready yet. So I practised for another couple of months. And went to Australia and then won four tournaments in a row.

I had a lot of injuries and pulled muscles in those years, though. All my muscles went soft. Your whole body changes when you have children and I found I had to work twice as hard.

I knew my legs wouldn't hold up for that long. Not many years were left before I'd be past my peak. The physical side was the great challenge at that time.

But I had this feeling that I still had a chance to win at Wimbledon. I didn't want having a baby to hold me back. That made me push myself harder. I wanted to prove to myself, and prove to other people, that life is not over after you have a child. You *must* carry on 110%!

Then shortly before the 1980 tournament I came down with a blood disorder and had to go to hospital. I wasn't able to play for six weeks. I kept thinking, what am I doing? I shouldn't be going to Wimbledon. I'm not ready. What on earth am I doing here? I was mad with myself. It was all so ridiculous.

But two weeks before Wimbledon began, I played in the final against Chris at Chichester. I lost in a three-set match, but I felt good. I didn't say anything but I felt quietly confident.

I practised well and was eager. When I got on the court, I couldn't wait for my opponent to serve. I actually was feeling aggressive – within myself. The one thing I kept telling myself was not that I was going to win the matches, but that I was not going to lose *this* match. It was nice to be on that high.

Kelly was with us. We took her everywhere and I saw her more than any working mother saw her child. Having her there, I really had to push but I was happier, too. A child teaches you to be less selfish; there's not so much thinking about yourself.

That took pressure off the tennis. As soon as I got off the court, I forgot the game completely because Kelly was there. She completely took over. I didn't have time to let things play on my mind, how badly I'd performed or whatever. That's when your confidence can suffer.

When you have kids, you don't have time to let yourself get down. You're always up. And you are much more aware of everything. Much more lively. You feel that because you have only a certain amount of time, you must put so much more into it.

When I won at Wimbledon the first time – in 1971, when I

43

was nineteen – I was just flitting through. I didn't really appreciate how big the tournament was. But in 1980 it meant so much more. I had reached my peak, mentally and physically. And I had a strong desire to win there again. I wanted that more than anything. You have to have that to get what you want from life.

CHAPTER FOUR

Achieving the Most with Your Talents

For half a dozen years, Ivan Lendl has been the most consistently successful tennis player in the world. Yet as Ivan himself is the first to acknowledge, he is not the best at every single aspect of his sport.

He does not volley as well as John McEnroe did in his prime. For sheer hand-speed, he is a hair less swift than Boris Becker. Yet season after season Ivan Lendl winds up at the top of the computer rankings and earnings list.

Lendl's secret is his shrewd understanding of his talents. He knows he can punish an opponent with pace. He won't tire. He can hit passing shots against anyone in the game. And while he can't be intimidated he *can* intimidate others, not by court melodramas but his ferocious concentration.

And he is totally honest about what his talents aren't. He cannot improvise like McEnroe; Lendl never invents the game as he goes along. And he is not a boom-boom serve and volleyer like Rod Laver or Arthur Ashe.

Knowing these weaknesses, he is able to shift the terms of the contest to make certain that his talents are used to best effect and his deficiencies minimized.

Self-knowledge is the key: whether you design skyscrapers or run the lunch counter, you cannot use your talents to their fullest unless you also know your weaknesses.

45

Finding Your Strength

All of us must play the hand we have been dealt. We can enhance natural talents with education, practice, concentration and will. But it is a dangerous fantasy to imagine that we can ignore our physical and mental limits.

Yet maximizing your talents is only half the battle, and in many cases the easiest part. Far more difficult is figuring out where your talents lie.

Athletes learn quickly, almost always as youngsters, and from then on coaches hone their skills. For most of us, though, matters aren't quite so clear-cut. We have a mixed-bag of abilities and probably none dominates.

We may take up a career because it runs in the family or a relative offers us a job. Or the field may seem glamorous, offering the excitement of travel.

Whatever you decide to try, don't be afraid to start again if the job disappoints you or your performance (be candid with yourself!) is disappointing. Motivation comes largely from success breeding success.

Major Hopping

I have known one man since he was a boy. As a student, he was the classic case of someone almost too well-rounded. He hovered between A-minus and B-plus in all his subjects. He was a solid but not a star athlete. He was creative though lacking the zeal of a true artist. When he took his exams before entering college, he scored almost identically on the maths and verbal sections.

In his freshman year he took mostly science courses. He thought he might concentrate on theoretical physics. (His father, a very practical man, told me that the physics part was fine, but the 'theoretical' would have to go.)

A year later, physics was out. The son didn't care for the nuts-and-bolts of it – the experiments with springs and pendulums that would lead to experiments with particle accelerators and

46

atom smashers. No, he realized now that what had drawn him to physics was the abstract part – formulae, proportions, ideal conceptions. What excited him about physics was actually mathematics, so he changed his major accordingly. (Practical Pop was less than thrilled. What did one do with a maths degree? Become a statistician? An actuary? A professor?)

Dad did not worry about that for long. Junior realized in his third year that while he loved the orderliness of maths, the coldness of numbers didn't appeal. What he really wanted, he decided, was a field that dealt in proportion, harmony and beautiful abstractions, yet brought these things on to a more human level. He decided to become an artist and changed courses again. (Where did we go wrong?, his practical parents asked.)

Ultimately, after a lot of money and seven semesters the young man found a focus. He decided to be an architect. He stuck with that and has thrived.

Though his father had despaired, considering his offspring a dilettante, I think the boy was doing a savvy and gutsy job discovering his talents and, not without pain, developing a commitment to one career.

Physics gave him a knowledge of how things held together. From maths came a sense of measure and order. From art, a developed eye and a disciplined hand.

I tell this story to reassure students who seem to feel that if they haven't decided on law school by the time they are sixteen, or haven't taken the prerequisites for an MBA in their freshman year, life is passing them by. Nonsense. Very few of us are equipped to make major decisions at such an age and usually more is lost than gained by trying to.

Life is school and finding one's talents is a lifelong process.

Reading Results

Reading results means reading yourself. Learn to understand when you've done well, when you've done badly, when you can improve and when you have reached your limits – learn just those four things and you're ahead of the pack.

A few years ago I heard a story that neatly illustrates the importance of reading results. An executive, looking for ways to drive home to his employees the value of feedback, took them bowling. For a while they bowled normally and the usual competitive dynamics developed. Everyone wanted to win. People helped their team-mates, discussed strategy and worked on their games.

Later in the evening the executive had a curtain drawn across the lanes; the bowling ball could roll through but the curtain blocked the sight of the pins. The employees could no longer see the results or keep score.

They soon grew bored. Teamwork fell apart. Improving their skills became meaningless when they couldn't assess the results. By the end of the evening everyone was annoyed and discouraged.

The executive apologized for causing frustration but he had made his point: bowling in the dark was the equivalent of a head of department never giving a subordinate a reading on performance or any credit. The employee couldn't keep score – and ultimately lost interest.

There are numerous ways to check your dark-of-night assessment of your performance and how well-suited you are for a particular job.

To begin with, ask your immediate boss for a frank appraisal. And listen to the answer. It is human nature to hear what we want to hear and block out the rest. And it is not uncommon for employees to believe they are more highly regarded than, in fact, they are. So be alert. Most bosses begin tactfully with the good news. Only later in the conversation will they get to what bothers them about your performance or suitability for the position.

These sessions clear the air *and* give you valuable advice to work on. You may pick up easy ways to put yourself on a faster track. And even if the critique is devastating, it is better to know your status than not to know. Being a flop at one thing isn't the end of life and it doesn't have to cause a crisis of confidence. We live in an age of specialization. Few of us are so narrowly gifted that there is only one thing we can do. There is a range of things we are good at and a range of things we are bad at.

Feedback is learning about yourself. Whether from your boss or from a friend, it will almost always point you in the right direction.

The Challenge of Smaller Victories

In life and in business, the chances of hitting a home run – winning a million on a sweepstake, masterminding a corporate takeover, creating a popular new magazine – are small. For each dramatic application of one's talents, there are thousands of smaller but no less demanding situations.

Among those things I value: a simple sales call, handled well, with tact and perfect timing; a beautifully crafted memo that conveys information using just the right number of words; a graciously handled social situation. Those skills can pay 110% dividends.

Concentrating on the megadeals when the stakes are high and known to all is relatively easy. Concentrating equally well on small things is, over time, what makes a winner.

People work better and feel better when they realize that their human-scale victories are appreciated. Letting them feel good about applying their talents to relatively small things will increase their confidence and competence when it comes to dealing with larger things.

Let me give an example of how this dynamic works at IMG. For a number of years our company has had a close relationship with the Royal & Ancient Golf Club of St Andrews. This venerable institution, the shrine of golf, was the originator of the British Open Championship. We have worked with the Royal & Ancient on this event, arranging broadcast rights, licensing deals and other aspects of marketing the tournament for many years.

The monies involved are substantial. But the benefits are not solely financial. Our association with the Royal & Ancient re-affirms our position in the sport of golf. We greatly value the business and are always looking for ways to enhance it.

A few years back, we had the notion of producing a hardcover annual about the British Open. We would organize the project and have the book written, and it would be published under the Royal & Ancient's imprimatur. The Club and IMG would be 50–50 partners in the proceeds.

The annual profits don't average all that much. In the larger scheme of things, they are barely worth the considerable time, trouble and manpower that goes into the project. Yet in another sense this seemingly small contribution is enormously impressive. Television coverage of an event is ephemeral. A book lasts.

There is no particular reason why the Royal & Ancient should remember from year to year the kind of job we do for it. Yes, there are accounting records but these are just numbers. A book preserves the feel, the quality of the experience. And the co-production of a book indicates something more than just a business relationship. It signifies an alliance. It suggests a tradition.

It is not stretching it to say that although we have a multifaceted relationship with the Royal & Ancient, one of the linchpins of the arrangement is this co-venture.

Winning Is a Separate Skill

Whether it is the resilience of Arnold Palmer or the consistency of Chris Evert, the performance of great athletes is a model for the rest of us who are striving to live at 110% intensity.

But let's descend for a moment from the lofty heights of world-class competitors to a humbler sphere of sport: club tennis. Anywhere there are a few courts, the same cast of characters seem to appear.

There is the former schoolboy star or collegiate player whose knees have gone and who wears an elbow brace, but who has wonderful match experience and court sense.

There is the earnest fellow who came to the sport late and spends a fair portion of his net worth (pun intended) on lessons.

There is the Given-Day Player, who always loses but claims that he can play a lot better on any given day.

And there is the quiet guy who always seems to win.

The chances are that this man has a dinky serve and questionable strokes. Ten people have better overhead and six have better passing shots. His volley is just so-so. In fact, people sit around analysing his game and no one can figure out why he can't be beaten. They cannot think of one single skill that he has and they don't. But that's because they are only looking for the skills that are *particular* to tennis.

They're not looking for the skill that is outside of tennis, applicable to all activities – a talent for winning.

You can work on your strokes until hell freezes over, and while you may improve your game you won't necessarily take the prize. Basic court sense will win you points but usually falls short of clinching the final set.

How does this dynamic apply in your business and personal life? Only in a million ways.

Take the brilliant woman hired as an editor of a magazine. She has standard editorial skills in abundance. She is a live wire on ideas for new stories. She works well with writers. She understands the magazine's readership and what it wants. Yet she languishes in a junior position, passed over for promotion, not just once but several times.

In her business winning is defined as getting pages into the magazine – making sure her stories get the space they deserve. This entails infighting at editorial meetings, some coaxing, some persuasion and occasionally some screaming.

The editor shrinks from this. Perhaps she hates to argue. Maybe she doesn't believe enough in the stories she's assigned and works on. Maybe she doesn't have sufficient trust in her own judgement.

The bottom line is that she does 95% of the work, then falters in the final steps, *the steps that lead to winning*.

Another example: A handsome, charming graduate of a top-tier business school goes to work for a major brokerage house. From day one this fellow has star performer written all over him. He looks great in his horn-rims and paisley tie. He's got an easy manner and everyone likes him. He has impressive academic credentials which he wears lightly so as not to intimidate people.

Yet for all his advantages, he turns out to be a mediocre performer. He has forgotten that winning is an ongoing process. You can't acquire a certain degree, a certain wardrobe, a certain manner, then coast. It just doesn't work that way. This man has become so comfortable with the idea of looking like a winner that he's lost his hunger for *being* a winner.

In club tennis this is the member with the lovely strokes, immaculate whites and perfect court demeanour. He loses 6–4, 6–4, and then acts like it's just a game and he doesn't really mind.

Another example: An executive in his early fifties changes companies, going from a large firm where he's No.3 to a smaller firm where he'll be No.2. This fellow has worked for many years, his kids have gone through college, his mortgage is paid off; he's well fixed financially. So his personal definition of winning is not primarily economic.

He wants to take this small, rather sleepy company and bring it into the late twentieth century; and he wants a shot at being CEO (Chief Executive Officer) before he retires. So he goes to this firm, gets it computerized, upgrades the sales staff, arranges the financing for some overdue capital improvements and, sure enough, the company takes off.

The executive naturally starts hankering for the promotion to CEO that will cap his career. But the company is a family-owned business and has been for generations. In the wings is a nephew in his middle-forties; he is a dolt but he is still the nephew. It becomes clearer and clearer to our friend that he is never going to run this outfit.

They'll pay lots of money to keep him – but, remember, money is no longer his personal way of measuring success. They'll keep him on as No.2 for ever, but at his stage of life job security is not an issue. He has fallen into a situation where he can do just fine, but where, by his own criterion for winning, he can't win.

You may say, 'Hey, this is a savvy businessman. Didn't he know what he'd be getting into joining a family business?' He should have known; and probably at some level he did know. But people have an astonishing capacity for self-deception. Being smart and shrewd when dealing with others is no guarantee that you won't be fooled by yourself.

Job skills are not an end in themselves. They are the raw material from which you shape your destiny.

Forget that and you may find yourself a nearly man. As they say in Hollywood, 'Close, but no cigar'.

Virginia Wade on 110% Commitment

In 1977, with the Queen in the Royal Box and all of Great Britain watching, Virginia Wade won the centenary Wimbledon at the age of thirty-one. Her victory was one of the most extraordinary sporting achievements I have ever seen. The British press has always made impossible demands of its sons and daughters in sport, but Virginia somehow transformed this pressure into a competitive edge. After so many close-but-no-cigar performances on the Centre Court, she truly had the home court advantage.

Winning that singles at Wimbledon was the high point of my tennis career. That was the occasion when I wasn't afraid to commit myself to 110%.

Until then I had always felt that if I started being single-minded about something, I would cut out a lot of the rest of my life. I had been somebody who spread myself widely. I had a surfeit of choices, rather than not enough choices. And that really is more difficult. Even on the tennis court I had too many choices.

So I had always found it difficult to commit myself. I was afraid to put myself on the line. Because once you do, you are then in a position to fail. Whereas if you always are dithering around, you can say, well, I wasn't 110%, which is absolutely true.

I had a fear of success more than a fear of failure. Deep down I believed that if I came through, I was then going to have to repeat the success, to live up to that level. That intimidated me.

I'd played tennis for a long time when suddenly it became apparent to me that I was committed to the game, that I should stop being a hypocrite and just go that extra step and say that I was committed. The moment you commit yourself, you do so much better. And you're much happier. People always have excuses for not committing themselves. They hide behind family or whatever.

I can pin my winning Wimbledon practically down to one hour and one day, a few months earlier. It was in the spring, and I knew I was getting on – what was I, thirty-one? And I was depressed that I'd never really performed at my best at Wimbledon. I mean how often does one perform at one's very best? Not very often.

You try to be 100% on the practice court with the possibility of being 85% in a match. In big matches, when there is real pressure, your performance level is going to come down. So your normal is probably only about 80% of your ability. Maybe twice a year you are close to 100%.

The pressure can sometimes bring a bit more out of you, but generally it takes a little away. I always felt at Wimbledon that it had lowered my performance. Pressure had not stimulated me to better things.

I was saying to a friend, given my age, how am I ever going to tackle Wimbledon again? Suddenly the question was thrown back at me – well, if you feel like that, why bother to play? Which immediately fired me up.

Very soon after that, I discovered that it was the centenary and that the Queen would be there. And it was like, my God, if the Queen's going to be at Wimbledon . . . she never goes. If I'm in the final, that means I've *got* to win. I know I'm not going to have another chance.

So I made a decision there and then that I was going to win. Everything was towards that goal. During the preparation and rehearsals I explored every possibility of what could happen. When you're out there you've got two hours in which to perform. You just have to put everything into the present moment. That is absolutely essential to achievement.

Steffi Graf may not have to go through all of this because it's so natural for her to think that she's a great player; she's a born No. 1. I was very talented, but I was missing a few ingredients. I had to work very hard in an intellectual way. Because I was very much an instinctive player, my mind was what needed the training. But I came into the tournament believing that I would win.

Once you've taken a match, you can't spend any time reflecting on that. You've got to start thinking about your next one. I was very businesslike about the matches and much more dedicated than usual at Wimbledon. I isolated myself. I admire people who do this automatically, who are so directed that their concentration never wavers.

My semifinal was the big match; I played Chris Evert. She was the No. 1 seed and had won Wimbledon twice before.

The moment my quarterfinal match was over, I spent all my waking hours focused on Chrissie. I knew exactly how I was going to play her. Exactly. I had rehearsed everything so that it was there. I didn't have to make any more choices on the court. I had made them. All I had to do was concentrate – and not worry.

The Queen, the centenary – those were added incentives that helped overcome the distractions. And I felt the crowd was pulling for me. But let me tell you, you still have to play well even when everybody's on your side! You still have to concentrate totally on the moment – that and the emotion carries you. You have to have all your senses heightened to be at your best.

55

That time at Wimbledon the motivation was greater than all the fears and distractions.

I met Betty Stove, who'd beaten Martina Navratilova and Sue Barker, in the final. Betty was always tough, but I had practically never lost to her. I had the psychological edge and I had to trust myself. The match ended 4–6, 6–3, 6–1.

Are You Afraid of the Commitment?

Like Virginia Wade, to win you have to make sacrifices – and you have to be realistic about them. You have to say to yourself, 'I want to be the world's best tennis player and this is what I am willing to give up to achieve that.'

When Bjorn Borg was winning five consecutive Wimbledon titles, his entire life was tennis. He would practise for four hours in the morning, play his match and then hole up in his room at the Holiday Inn in Swiss Cottage in London with his girlfriend, his parents and his coach, Lennert Berglin, ordering meals from room service and watching television, waiting for the next match.

Jean-Claude Killy once surprised me by admitting that he didn't know how to dance. He had been too busy skiing to learn. 'In fact,' he said, 'I haven't seen a summer in years. When it's winter in Europe, I am skiing in the Alps. When it is summer, I am skiing in South America.'

America's Cup skipper Dennis Conner is blunter than most on the subject. 'Winning is not for everyone,' he says. 'You have to be a little abnormal. If you want to be the very best at anything you have to make sacrifices. You cannot be the world's best golfer *and* the world's best businessman, the world's best father *and* the world's best President. You must give up things to get there, whether it is as a writer or a movie producer or President of the United States. You think he's *normal*?'

To become a world-class yachtsman, Conner settled for being a mediocre father: 'I'm not proud to say it, but my family hasn't been No. 1. You have to draw up your priorities. My wife knew

56

the situation before we married. We postponed our wedding three times because I had to go sailing.'

That is a Faustian bargain many people are not willing to acknowledge, let alone make. It also helps, of course, if you have a heroic and understanding wife or husband.

The sad part is not that people cannot make the sacrifices, but rather that they deceive themselves about *why* they aren't making the commitment. Usually it's because they have settled on another commitment where they cannot be judged as harshly, where they cannot be exposed to failure, where there are no objective criteria for success.

Rather than totally commit themselves to what may involve tough competition, many people say, 'I'd rather spend more time with my family.' There's nothing wrong with that. That's a legitimate trade off. It's tough to do both at 110%.

But what's really going on here? Is the sacrifice too much? Or is coasting along simply an easier choice to make? I think a lot of people deceive themselves this way. They're not so much afraid of the sacrifice as of making the commitment to succeed. If someone told them, 'I can guarantee that you will get the promotion you have always wanted, but you can see your wife and children only twice in the next six months,' if they looked deep into their hearts and were honest with themselves, many people might make that trade off.

None of us can guarantee that we will get what we want from life. But unless you passionately want to succeed, you will never be a winner.

Dennis Conner on 110% Commitment

Dennis Conner has two distinctions in yacht racing, one painful, one glorious. In 1983 he became the first American in history to lose the America's Cup. Four years later, in Fremantle, Australia, he won it back. Conner is the first total-commitment yachtsman. He was willing to campaign for two years with two boats. He brought sophisticated technology and exhaustive pre-race testing of crew and equipment to the sport. He taught himself the delicate art of raising financing. Dennis is certainly a colourful, dashing skipper, and I don't think anything surprises him on the water. I have yet to meet a more thoroughly prepared competitor in any sport.

I remember only once being able to get 110% out of myself. It was at the Star Class World Championship in Kiel, Germany, in 1977, and I won every race, scoring five straight firsts, against eighty-nine boats. That had never been done and probably never will be again. It was one of those times when things went exceedingly well.

In sailing something less than 100% is usually good enough. The 90% or 95% level can win in my particular sport. It is very difficult to sail a perfect race. There are so many ifs. The wind is fluctuating. There are waves to go over. There are just so many permutations.

It is different from having to sit down and negotiate with Lee Iacocca or the Japanese – to summon up your brilliance at one particular moment.

My style is not to rely on talent and ability but to bludgeon the competition, to work harder than the other guy. No stone left unturned. Attention to detail is how I get there. You can win with tremendous talent. But I combine mostly effort with some talent.

You have to have some talent. It's part of the pie. If it's basketball, it's a large part of the pie. That's a sport where there is a big premium on talent. The world's best athletes are out there duking it out, so attitude, in this one case, is not as important.

All sports are not created equal. A lot of them are physical. Sailing is more mental. With the America's Cup, raising the money and having the technology is more important than having a good crew.

You need to know your deficiencies. You have to face reality. It is important to excel at your strengths because that momentum

58

will carry over into other areas. I don't dwell on my problems because that would be negative. But you must cover yourself.

You must establish priorities. In 1983 after I lost the America's Cup to Australia, I could have rationalized and pretended that I didn't care. The hurt was there. It took a while to recover and come to grips with the fact that winning the Cup back was a high priority.

Some people tell you it's beneficial to lose occasionally. I wouldn't recommend losing to anyone. But I have a special place in the hearts of a lot of people because I went through a particularly devastating loss. I find presidents of corporations and decision-makers enjoy speaking with someone who's been in the firing line just like they have. They have empathy with what it is like to lose the America's Cup, the first time in its 132-year history, and then suck it up and win the Cup back.

I learned from my mistakes. In 1983, we got beaten by a faster boat. I didn't do as good a job of checking out the competition as I should have. I have a maxim that I should have followed: You Snooze, You Lose. Reading the competition is one of the parts of the America's Cup pie. I didn't cover all my bases. I didn't know the Australians had the secret keel or how fast it was until it was too late to respond. So they had a weapon just too good for us.

In 1987 I did a much better job of watching the competition; and I relied more on technology. Four years before I had relied on natural talent and the seat of the pants.

The race is not always to the swift. You have to have a good plan tactically. You can run the four-minute mile and get boxed in at the wrong time. Life works the same way. The ladies don't necessarily go for the best-looking guy.

But even more important, you cannot achieve your top abilities unless you have a self-image that will allow you to get there. Self-image serves as a governor. On a car, it's the accelerator. It governs your performance in life.

I'm sure Mark McCormack, the golfer, feels some days that he shouldn't be competing against Jack Nicklaus or Arnold

Palmer on the golf course. But if he's playing you and me, he has no concerns. It's the big-dog syndrome.

We are affected by self-image every day and every way – brushing our teeth, in how we dress, how we perform on the golf course or on a sailboat. Self-image affects how we operate – with other people and in our personal lives.

There are ways to bolster your self-esteem. One is by having a very vivid imagination. Or you can improve your self-image by real-life drama – as the result of how you actually do out there on the race course. I use both approaches.

You have to know how to use a vivid imagination. I can gauge what amount of adrenalin, what excitement level works best for me. So if I'm feeling down and I want to get excited, I think about something that will excite me, that makes me feel good. That I'm a winner. That I'm standing on the steps getting my Olympic medal and hearing the *Star Spangled Banner*. [Conner won the bronze medal in the Tempest class at the 1976 Games.] Or I'm coming to the finish line, winning the seventh race of the America's Cup. I think about things like that – good, positive reinforcement. If I'm too excited, I focus on something that will calm me.

If you want to reach the top rank in anything, you must feel good about your chances of success.

The three most important things are: *Attitude, Attitude* and *Attitude*.

The Elements of Winning

There are numerous ways to snatch defeat from the jaws of victory – to fall short of winning even when the machinery to succeed is all in place.

1. Know which battles you have to win

Nobody wins all the time – every point in a tennis match or every hole in a golf tournament. No business person pulls off a coup on every deal, and the greatest salesmen come up empty a fair proportion of the time. One of the skills that distinguishes a winner is an instinct for knowing when he can afford to lose and when he must win. That permits him to focus his efforts.

Choose your Must-Wins with care. Concentrate on the essentials and plot your course. Don't be distracted by friends, enemies or your own emotions.

2. Love to Win. Don't hate to lose

The difference is subtle but loving to win and hating to lose are not the same. One is driven by joy. The other is inspired by fear.

In thoroughbred racing, champions are 'born to run'. There is a sheer animal vigour in finishing first. Nothing interferes with that single goal. That same purity of intention and clarity of purpose is found in humans skilled in the art of winning.

Hating to lose muddies the waters. Fear breeds misjudgement. Instead of concentrating 110% on your goal, you waste effort worrying about what the other guy is doing.

Hating to lose can lead to a big mistake. There is a major New York developer who has an enormous ego and can't stand to be topped in a bid. He is probably as knowledgeable as anyone on earth about what pieces of Manhattan should cost. Nevertheless, a couple of years ago, when a particularly valuable and visible parcel came up for sale, he made a megamillion mistake – a mistake that left others in the industry astonished. He bid so much for this property that he couldn't possibly avoid losing money. Other heavy-hitters were also bidding and the thought of not being top dog was appalling to this fellow. So he won the bid and probably lost $200 million.

3. Be relentless, not malicious

In pre-fight interviews boxers make a point of how much they hate each other. Whether this is hype or whether the men really do need to work up a personal dislike to be able to go out and pummel each other, I don't presume to say.

In most competitions, personal animosity is not the issue and frequently it is downright counter-productive. Even in most head-to-head sports, you are not really battling an opponent – you are matching something you do against something he does.

Consider tennis. You hit a shot; your opponent hits a shot. Now what is it you are actually hitting? The ball – not the other player.

4. Depersonalize the contest

Bjorn Borg was a master at this. His icy court demeanour was his own brand of relentlessness – one devoid of malice. Borg neither liked nor disliked an opponent. He was there to do one thing and one thing only: to hit the ball perfectly every time it appeared on his side of the net.

What happened on the other side and who it happened to was simply not his concern.

I stress this because, in situations where the contest is more abstract, there is a tendency to overpersonalize competition. If you are General Motors, you don't 'combat' imports by taking a crowbar to a Honda. You do it by outperforming the other side.

At IMG we have a number of competitors who want our clients. And there are people whose clients we want. There are companies trying to elbow in on the events we run. We'd be stupid if we didn't realize those companies were out there or if we denied they were eager to get our business.

We would be equally mistaken, however, if we ascribed too much importance to battling them or, above all, if we put the contest on a personal level. Our energy would then be wasted in reacting to our rivals instead of acting positively on our own. If that same time was devoted to improving our service, thinking up innovative programmes and doing an excellent job for our clients, there would be no need to worry about the other guys. We would have outperformed them.

Personalize the contest and egos start to conflict with sound professional judgement.

Martina Navratilova on 110% Commitment

For sheer athleticism, Martina Navratilova may be the most talented woman of the modern era (and one of the more misunderstood by the general public). She is warm, funny and extremely smart. Because she tends to wear her heart on her sleeve, she may be more vulnerable mentally than Chris Evert and Steffi Graf, her principal rivals. But that is a positive quality, too. Martina's fame and wealth have put her in circles where it is very difficult to be genuine and retain your humanity. She has managed to do that – and remain a great champion.

A lot of people get hung up thinking, 'I'll be happy when I reach this goal.' When I won my first Wimbledon in 1978, that was the case. With the trophy in hand, I thought the whole world was going to stop and admire me for what I'd done. But the world couldn't have cared less. It was the headline story one day and the next day there were new headlines. The bottom line was that I had to keep playing and keep winning.

The concentration that had given me that Wimbledon victory was what I needed to take me higher. You must have the ability to focus on the present and the process, to commit yourself 110%.

I remember the second round of Wimbledon in 1989. Everything that could be going against me in a match *was* against me. I was playing an Australian, a qualifier named Kristine Radford whom I had beaten in Birmingham a couple of weeks before.

We were assigned Court Two, which is notorious for upsets because the bounces are really bad. We started the match at seven o'clock, when it was already too dark to play, and the setting sun was in my eyes. There was a shadow moving across the court. We both knew it was too late to play. Hardly anybody was watching. Then the sun went down and we couldn't see a thing.

I was down a set and 3–1, break. I hadn't broken a serve yet and I was in trouble. Somehow I had to find a way to break

63

Kristine's serve and win the set. With one set each we could finish the match the next day. So it was up to me to find a way to win that set, but it wasn't going to be easy.

I had to take myself back to basics and concentrate on just one thing, the ball. If the problem was that I wasn't having an easy time getting the serve back to her, I had to focus on getting that serve back and nothing else. I told myself, 'It doesn't matter where, just get it back to her and then you can play the point. Instead of trying to play it fancy, instead of trying to hit it down the line or across the court, just try to get her to hit the ball again.'

I had been worrying about the other things that were happening – I couldn't see, the bounces were lousy, it was late at night and getting cold. Instead, I had to play the ball – not the other player, not the match, not the crowd. *The ball*. It sounds simple, but that's what I did and it worked. I won the set and we broke until the next day. Then things improved and I beat her as I had planned to.

What I had done that evening was to simplify the match. To focus on the one thing I had to do to get where I needed to be.

If you think about the implications of what you're trying to do, if you spend time worrying about all the outside influences and all the things that could get in the way, you'll be overwhelmed.

Some days, no matter how hard you try, it just isn't happening. You just aren't getting what you need to get. Then you have to retreat and look very closely at what is wrong.

It's not that it is too late at night to be playing. It's not that there have been lots of upsets on Court Two. Those things are not what's beating you. It is that you are not hitting that ball back to your opponent. So put the rest aside and hit the ball back – if you don't, the other things aren't going to matter anyway.

Of course, you have to work on all aspects of the game – you have to take the wind, the sun, the bounces and everything into account in every match. But that's what practice and preparation are for. You practise until the adjustments happen automatically during the match. Then when the wind is blowing this way and the ball is coming at you that way, in an instant you know what to do. It has become a habit. By working with coaches to bring as many things under control as I can, I've made it possible to concentrate on every twist and turn of the game.

That night I knew I had to get out of the past, out of the serves I hadn't been able to get back and out all the things that were wrong about the match.

And I had to get out of the future, out of worrying about beating Kristine the next day.

I had to get into the present, into that ball coming over the net.

Doing that takes concentration, which I've worked hard to learn. Because of my athletic talent, sometimes I've been able to get away with letting my mind be all over the place. Chris Evert always knew she couldn't afford to let her mind wander. She's not as good an athlete as I am, so if she had had my head, she wouldn't have got anywhere! And her game dictates maximum concentration, because her game plan is the methodical destruction of her opponent by not missing anything. Mine is just a wham-bam here, a dink there, a top-spin lob over there. As a more artistic player, I could get away with blowing off a couple of points and then getting back in with a big serve.

Watching Chris play, I could see how sometimes I was beating myself by getting too upset about something. Maybe I had hit a bad shot and was still moaning about it three games later. So that one shot had cost me three games. Chris would never dwell on that – she is just very good at staying in the present and focusing on what has to be done.

I've had to work to get this kind of focus to become a habit, to get to the point where in a match my attention is very sharp, very precise on exactly what is happening.

When I'm on the court, I am alone. The preparation has been done and it is up to me to deliver. If I'm not ready, nobody can help me. I have to figure it out myself.

When I first started working on my head and my focus, it was exhausting. I had to concentrate on concentrating, until concentrating became a habit for me. If I hit a bad shot, I had to figure out why I missed it and try to improve the next time, but then put it behind me.

You have to when you're in a match – the small things and the big ones. Everything from the serve you missed a few minutes ago to the big matches you know you should have won in the past. In 1989 I knew I had the US Open in the bag. I should have won that match, but I didn't. It just wasn't working for me that day. It still hurts me that I lost. But if I think about that when the ball is coming over the net in my next match, what good does that do? Should I make myself lose another match just because I lost the US Open?

What I've found is that I enjoy the process more than most people, and that has helped me. I enjoy the match while I'm playing it; I don't just enjoy it after I've won and seen my picture in the paper.

CHAPTER FIVE

110% Authority

If you want to be a great boss, look at parents. Good mothers and fathers are natural bosses.

They know how to motivate, educate and discipline. They are masters at delegating responsibilities and establishing priorities.

They are wizards at allocating limited resources.

They are consistent.

They know when to step into a situation and when to stay out.

They are there when you need them.

Steve Ross, the chairman of Warner Communications and now chairman of Time Warner, once explained in the *New Yorker* how he dealt with his executives: 'You have to be solid, you have to be a rock, you have to be a father – you have to encourage them to make mistakes, and they will, because they know you're there.'

I don't want to overplay this parent/boss analogy – and I certainly don't want to suggest that we start treating employees as 'children'. But a lot of people have trouble being the boss. They confuse being bosslike with being bossy.

The most important duty of a boss is to motivate people. Build them up when they're down and, conversely, knock them down a peg or two when they begin to rest on their laurels.

Parents don't have to be taught this. It is intuitive. If our child has done something well at school, we praise him, but part of us is on alert; we don't want the child to be smug or self-satisfied. So along with the praise, we may joke about a tiny flaw or remind him that a few of his peers did just as well. We bring him down a notch or two, so he can scale greater heights the next time.

Conversely, if a child has done something stupid – for instance, getting separated from us in a crowd – our impulse might be to reprimand him so that he will never do it again. But instinctively we stifle our anger. We comfort the frightened child – and save the lecture for a more appropriate moment.

I remember an airline commercial a few years back that parodied this motivation technique. It showed a weary football team in the locker room at half-time. The coach, at fever pitch, was sketching miscues and new plays on the blackboard, exhorting his players to do better during the second half.

Finally, a beefy, mud-splattered lineman looked up and asked, 'Coach, aren't we ahead by twenty-seven points?'

The coach paused and replied, 'That's exactly what I mean.'

Knowing when to be tough and when to be tender is a discipline that many bosses seem to leave at home. Parents who are smart enough to ease up on a frightened child somehow lose this common sense when they enter the workplace. Instead of supporting employees after a setback, they belittle and berate them.

I think the following qualities are what distinguish someone with 110% authority from the rest of the pack:

1. Good bosses must be great simplifiers

They must take complicated situations and reduce them to their essence.

John Havlicek, the Boston Celtics star, once told me, 'What made Red Auerbach such a great basketball coach was his ability to simplify. People could always understand what he said.'

Other coaches install complicated 'continuity offences' with dozens of plays and variations, but Auerbach's system consisted of only eight plays, each with an option. Auerbach figured that if the set play didn't work, you went to the option. If the option failed, it was a bad play. You didn't deserve to score.

Other coaches teach fancy techniques like the 'crossover step' and the 'reverse pivot' to improve rebounding. Not Auerbach. All he would say on the subject was, 'Make sure your man doesn't get the rebound.' If all Celtic players did their job, the ball would end up in Celtic hands.

In the mid-1970s we had a crisis in our tennis division. Our client, John Newcombe, the top-ranked player in the world and the anchor of our fledgeling division, insisted on meeting with me.

The moment Newcombe walked into my office, I could see that he wasn't happy.

'What's wrong?' I asked.

Newcombe made a convincing case for quitting our organization. He felt that we were neglecting him, taking him for granted.

He was a Wimbledon champion three times over, he had won the US Open championship twice and he was No. 1 in the computer rankings. Newcombe was the hottest property in the fastest-growing sport, and we weren't making enough money for him. Projects seemed to be falling through the cracks. He didn't feel he was getting the undivided attention he deserved – and had earned – and he was thinking about finding other representation.

'You're absolutely right,' I told him. 'We have dropped the ball. You deserve better. I can understand why you want to quit us.' We shook hands. I wished him well, and he walked out the door.

Within seconds I was on the phone to the executive who was running our tennis division. I could have replayed the entire conversation. I could have explained how crucial Newcombe was to the tennis division. I could have reviewed point by point the errors we had made. I could have reminded the executive how embarrassing this would be. I could have pointed out how this might complicate many projects in progress.

But I didn't. I told him, 'John Newcombe was just in my office and he's quitting. I want you to become John Newcombe's best friend.'

In other words, I kept it simple. I didn't see any advantage in weighing the executive down with the dire consequences of losing Newcombe or rehashing what went wrong. That would only distract and demoralize him.

All I did was point him in the right direction. It was up to him to figure out the details.

Within twenty-four hours the executive was aboard a plane to Arizona, where Newcombe was playing in a tournament. For the next three weeks our man glued himself to Newcombe. He followed him on the circuit, watched his matches, hung around the locker room, gently tried to make him reconsider. He assured Newcombe, in word and deed, that he would personally handle his affairs.

The net result is that, fifteen years later, John Newcombe is still our client and a happy one.

2. Good bosses are great informers

To a good boss, information has three functions: to inform, to instruct, to motivate. Motivating is the tricky part.

I used to believe that you could never tell your employees too much. If you were totally open with them about what was going on in the company, they would be more open with you. It seemed like a fair exchange to me.

But I soon learned that there is a problem with too much communication. For one thing, if you give people good news that they had no hand in creating, they often get jealous. Even worse, if you give them bad news in areas where they cannot have an impact, they get demoralized.

I once wrote a memo to our executives that listed fifteen potential disasters in the coming year. I didn't differentiate between big and small items. My 'disasters' ran the whole gamut from a client who might leave us, to a tennis player with a back injury, to an oil crisis that was forcing corporations to scale back their involvement in sports, to soaring airline ticket prices which meant that we would have to be extremely prudent with travel expenses.

I hoped this litany would inspire people to tighten their belts and get ready for a rough ride.

Unfortunately, it had the opposite effect. I remember one executive telling me he was so depressed by the memo that he came away thinking, 'Things are so bad that no matter what we do, we can't correct it. The year will be awful. The company is going down the drain.'

Nowadays, I am extremely careful how I transmit that sort of information to people. I consider how an individual will deal with it. If bad news paralyses a person, I'll understate my pessimism, even if it means being less than candid. How I deliver the information is not nearly as important as how it is received.

Information that doesn't push people forward and get them on the right track is needless information.

3. Good bosses stay in the trenches

People make mistakes when they become the boss. They make sweeping changes rather than slow, measured ones. They criticize their predecessor. They knock down previous policies. They establish goals and expectations that are impossible to live up to.

But by far the biggest mistake a boss can make is to 'act like the boss'.

Several years ago people in our company convinced me that one of our executives in Japan was so good that we had to put him in charge of sales in our Tokyo office. Unfortunately, none of us envisioned that the new title would go to his head. His personality changed. Rather than being sensitive to the possibility that his peers would be offended by his promotion, he decided to rub it in. He started flaunting his authority by playing favourites. He funnelled the most attractive projects to cronies. He redecorated his office. He did everything possible to demonstrate that he had pulled himself out of the trenches.

71

It is apparent now that what he should have done with his new title – especially in Japan where consensus and team play is the norm – is to have gone *deeper* into the trenches to make things work. He should have been more responsive, more helpful, more of a team player. That would have confounded everyone's expectations, allayed their fears and made them more productive.

A good boss does not have to boss. He helps people so that eventually they won't need him. If he is there beside them rather than above them, then when success comes everyone will feel that it is their success too and that it happened naturally.

4. A good boss doesn't need to be a star

The toughest part of being a boss is recognizing your strengths and letting others cover for your weaknesses.

In this regard, perhaps the best boss I've ever heard of was the editor-in-chief of a successful weekly magazine. I was being interviewed by a veteran reporter from the magazine when the two of us began chatting about his boss. Most of the editors I've met tend to be classic 'idea' people. Ideas are their stock in trade. They can think up a dozen just by walking down the street and observing people. I told the reporter how much I admired his magazine and how lucky he was to be working for such a creative editor. As I complimented him on several stories that I considered particularly clever, a puzzled look came over his face.

'You've got it all wrong,' he said. 'I've been in the magazine business for thirty years and he is the first boss I've ever met who doesn't have any ideas. He knows good writing, he knows pictures, he knows what people want. But when it comes to generating story ideas, he lets us do that. Every Monday, he walks around the office and tells each of us to have seven new ideas on his desk by Wednesday.'

My admiration for his boss rose another notch. Anyone who can produce a successful magazine fifty-two times a year without

72

one idea of his own must know the importance of being a boss rather than a star.

Soften the Sting of Criticism

The trouble with berating your vice-president or your teenager is that the situation is inherently belittling. There is an implication that you know all the answers and they don't. If that is precisely the point you are seeking to convey, your criticism will be to no good purpose. You can skip this chapter.

The inept use of criticism is among the most common causes of conflict in the workplace, ahead of mistrust, personality conflicts, even disputes over power and dissatisfaction with salaries.

It is often more effective to make your views known in ways so subtle that people don't realize they are being criticized.

Ask questions before demanding answers

Instead of telling someone, 'You blew it!', calmly take them through a series of questions (implying that you don't have all the answers): 'Did you ever consider?', 'What if you had told Mr Smith?' Usually this results in something of a Socratic dialogue and your employee or your offspring reaches the desired conclusion – and thinks it's his idea. Now obviously if you are enraged and the cords are standing out on your neck, this approach doesn't have a prayer of success. Anger has its uses, but rarely when your purpose is useful criticism.

Criticism should be timely

There is nothing worse than blaming someone for ancient trespasses that everyone but you has long forgotten. Criticize someone only when the mistake is fresh in everyone's mind and the evidence is beyond dispute.

73

Focus on the crime, not the criminal

A hallmark of effective criticism is that it deals with what a person has done, not with the person. It doesn't treat poor performance as a character flaw. There's a world of difference between saying, 'That wasn't smart!' and 'You're stupid!'

Be selective

The occasion when you hold back on criticism and let the perpetrator off the hook makes as much, if not more, of an impact than the times when the critic lets it all out. The best bosses and fathers don't comment on every goof. They pick their moment.

Be economical

The effectiveness of criticism is not measured by how long you take to deliver it. And the longer you talk the more likely you are to say something that you will regret.

Deliver it in person

Criticizing people in writing rather than in person is a lot like trying to be funny in a memo. You can't predict how the reader will take it, except that you can be sure your comments will sound much harsher than you intended. Worse yet, they are now a matter of formal record which you may live to regret.

Let them do most of the work

When it comes to criticism, your child and your employee often have a better idea of what they did wrong than you do. So it's a good idea to let them do some of the work for you.

I know one executive who, before he carpets an employee,

has his secretary warn them, 'I've hardly ever seen the boss this mad before . . .' on the theory that by the time the employee makes it to the boss's office, he or she will be filled with more fear, guilt and self-recrimination than a lecture from the CEO could ever inspire.

I don't fully endorse this approach, but it is comforting to know that some people can be harsher on themselves than a boss ever could be.

Give them a way out

The best criticism doesn't lead to a dead end. It leaves open an escape route.

When Mimi Sheraton was the respected and feared restaurant critic of the *New York Times*, she turned out to dislike many of her boss's favourite restaurants. This put her esteemed executive editor, A. M. Rosenthal, in an awkward position. On the one hand, Sheraton was entitled to her views and it was important that she be perceived as unbiased and beyond arm-twisting by anyone. On the other hand, the socially minded Rosenthal still had to show his face at some of the targets of Sheraton's vigorous prose.

Rosenthal's solution was clever and speaks volumes about how to deliver fair criticism. He didn't muzzle Sheraton. He couldn't have done so and kept her as a critic. Instead, he convinced her that if she was going to lambast an establishment, she could score more points *if she felt sorry about doing it.*

'Instead of writing, "The place is terrible,"' Rosenthal suggested, 'You could say, "It's too bad the place is terrible."' Even the severest criticism will often be acceptable if you appear sympathetic.

Let Your People Go – with Your Blessings

There comes a time when an employee you value highly is offered a good opportunity outside your organization. The person will be able to stretch and grow in unexpected ways and receive many thousands more than you can pay him.

Often this person comes to you for advice. Often he is apprehensive about the challenge of the new job and isn't at all certain he wants to leave, especially if you have become his mentor. As hard as it is to do, this is the time to put the employee's future ahead of your own or your company's. Encourage him to take the outside offer if it is the sort of position you wouldn't – or shouldn't – have passed up at the same stage of your career. Honestly evaluate the offer from the employee's point of view, *not your own*. Ask the kind of probing questions that you would ask yourself if you were the one considering such a move. This helps your employee to think more wisely about the important decision he faces. And if you believe he ought to take the job, say so.

Only goodwill can come of this. Not only do you earn respect and make a lifelong friend but somewhere down the line he is going to return the favour and goodwill, not just to you, but to your company.

Don't Forget to Mention Your Bad Deals

When you have only a limited amount of time to impress someone, it is human nature to try to put your best foot forward. But sometimes people get carried away. They are so intent on highlighting all their wonderful achievements that they forget how disarming it can be to spotlight one or two things that went wrong.

For example, one of the wealthiest, most successful businessmen I know is constantly telling me (and anyone else who will listen) how great things are. He is perpetually recounting the wonderful transactions he's pulled off – how he made $30 million on an oil deal or how a bank stock went up 82 points after he bought it. He is an unrelenting optimist and an incorrigible braggart. It's part of his charm.

Yet I can't help thinking how much more refreshing he would be if occasionally he mentioned the deals that went sour, if he could find it within himself to say, 'You won't believe this, but I bought this building for $700,000 and the next day it was condemned.'

Someone who did that would grow by multiples in my estimation. It would make him appear more fallible, more human and more honest – because nobody wins 100% of the time.

This self-effacing quality is valuable in all pursuits, whether you are a millionaire or a youngster just getting started in life. If you bring up events that went wrong, where you really messed up, people will be more inclined to believe your description of the things that went right.

Candour creates trust, not suspicion.

For proof, just look around your office. To whom do you relate more easily? The boastful executive whose property values have soared since he moved into his beautiful house, who is always making a killing in the stock market and whose children only get straight As? Or is it the quiet overachiever who tempers every bit of good fortune in his life by mentioning, often with humour, the downside?

I suppose people in selling situations are reluctant to spotlight their mistakes because they feel that that somehow paints them as incompetent. But there really is nothing to lose. After all, nobody is going to ask you about your disasters so it is all the more impressive when you bring them up yourself.

I saw this dynamic at work early in my career with Arnold Palmer. By any definition, Arnold has been one of the most successful sports personalities of the past three decades. If anyone had a licence to boast every once in a while, it would be him. But even in his twenties and thirties, Arnold had an instinctive grace and humility that people could relate to.

When interviewers and fans would ask him to sum up his year, as they constantly did, he could easily have answered by listing the superlatives: 'Well, I averaged 69.8 a round, I won two tournaments, one major, and more than $200,000.' But invariably Arnold would poke fun at himself.

On one occasion, when fans swarmed around him before an exhibition match, I heard him respond by describing in delicious detail how he shot a 12 on one hole in the Los Angeles Open. The fans did not walk away thinking about what a poor golfer Palmer was. Instead, they saw the very appealing qualities of the man. They saw he was human and fallible, just like them. And they saw the honesty and total lack of self-satisfaction that made him a champion.

Be human, and be honest. Among all your glorious victories, remember to mention a few defeats.

All Meetings Are Boring – Except, Of Course, Yours

I'm always being told that meetings are the bane of life, and they are – if you fail to get 110% from *everyone* present. In order to do that you have to confront a fact: meetings are potentially boring – except, of course, the ones *you* call to order.

A major reason for complaining about meetings is that the people chairing them are having more fun than the people attending them. This is also true of speeches, where the enthusiasm of the speaker is rarely matched by the audience. That is one reason an experienced public speaker removes his wristwatch before a speech and places it where he can keep track of the time. No matter how gripping his oratory, he knows that time moves a lot faster for him than it does for the audience.

It doesn't matter what sort of meeting you convene. Whether you are addressing shareholders on the fate of a corporation or a parents' association on whether soda machines should be permitted in the school cafeteria, the person running the meeting will have a more compelling reason to be there than the people attending.

78

There are all sorts of reasons for attending meetings. Most people are there out of some form of self-interest, to hear how the subject under discussion affects them. Some attend to voice their opinion; they don't seriously care what anyone else has to say. Some attend to lend moral support to a friend or colleague. Still others show up because someone asked or forced them to go.

That is why it is so important for you, if you're running the meeting, to minimize any factors that could lessen an audience's interest. Some factors to consider:

1. Time

The most important element in any meeting is time. When does the meeting start? When does it end? You would be amazed at how few people give sufficient thought to this.

During the peak years of his career, the classical pianist Vladimir Horowitz elected to perform only on Sunday afternoons at four o'clock. He avoided evenings or weekdays because he did not want a tired audience that had worked all day and rushed through dinner to attend his concerts. He wanted the audience well rested and not distracted – as it would be on Sunday afternoons.

Wilful scheduling? Not a bit of it. Horowitz turned his legions of fans into a 110% audience.

Let's figure out why. Rule One: Never have meetings at times usually devoted to something else – for example, to playing golf or tennis. This is the major flaw of many corporate meetings. They are held in resort facilities, ostensibly to minimize distractions. No mail, no faxes, no ringing phones. Unfortunately, the way these meetings are often structured – work in the morning, play in the afternoon – only maximizes the distractions. The end result is that people unconsciously rush through the work session and let their minds wander to the golf course or tennis court.

Rule Two: People must be comfortable during a long meeting. The timing of a meeting has to be consistent with people's mood, with their attention span and body chemistry.

Every year I hold a week of meetings with three dozen or so of our company's top executives at Whatley Manor outside London. Each day is divided into four working sessions that get shorter as the day goes on.

The day begins with coffee and juice as we walk into a 7 a.m. session. That meeting lasts three hours and then a full breakfast is served. Those who don't want breakfast can take a walk, read the newspaper, confer with colleagues or get their European phone calls done at the best time of the day. This is the longest session, and the shortest break.

We reconvene ninety minutes later for two and a half hours, from 11.30 until 2 p.m., followed by a two-hour break for lunch. Again, people who don't want lunch can do whatever they want. This break is designed for rest and for placing calls to the United States, where the business day has just begun.

The next session, lasting two hours, starts at 4 p.m., followed by a break from six to eight o'clock.

At eight we go into dinner, where the staff have been instructed to serve briskly. After the main course, we start our evening discussions, which last from roughly 8.30 to ten o'clock.

That is nine hours of meetings, three meals and three breaks. This goes on for six days. It is a tiring week for me, since I'm running the meetings, but the progressively shorter sessions somehow seem to ease the fatigue for everybody. The comfortable surroundings and the carefully timed breaks that let people stay in touch with the real world minimize the feeling that we are caught up in a meeting marathon.

The optimum hour for a meeting is not necessarily the obvious one. A little imagination goes a long way to improving meetings.

Somehow, asking people to meet at 7 a.m. has a different effect from calling them together at five o'clock in the afternoon. The early meeting may be unusual, but it imparts a sense of urgency to the subject at hand that you don't always get in meetings called at the end of the workday, when people are winding down and not as concerned about time.

Intelligent timing applies to almost any meeting, in or out of the workplace.

For example, if you have to talk with a contractor who is renovating your house, when would you schedule the meeting? Most working people schedule it in the evening, after work when it is convenient for both parties. Yet the evening hours are probably the worst time to meet. Both of you are tired from a full day's work. Both of you would rather be relaxing with friends or family. And an evening meeting at your home has a vague, open-ended quality. It may last longer than either of you prefer. You would be better off meeting first thing in the morning, when you are fresh and eager to get on with your busy day.

Given the choice, I would schedule almost any meeting early in the day rather than later. And I have a hunch that even public meetings would run more efficiently – and certainly with less rancour – if they were scheduled at 7.30 a.m. before the town's citizens went to work.

2. Brains instead of ego

Your biggest challenge in running a meeting is to get people to bring their brains to the table and check their ego at the door.

My solution is to pay close attention to self-serving statements. People have a tendency to toot their own horn in meetings, and this tendency only increases as the size of the meeting grows. I realize that if an executive has done something wonderful, it's only natural to want to tell the world about it. But meetings are rarely the appropriate forum.

I don't know how many times I've heard executives begin their report in a meeting by recounting how they took over a sick division and nursed it back to profitability. These self-serving statements are designed to impress people, but they often have the opposite effect – because everyone already knows what the executive has done and they think he's a boor for bragging about it.

I don't have a problem congratulating people in meetings, especially when it prevents them from congratulating themselves.

Quite often, I will introduce an executive by saying, 'Before Joe starts, let me tell you where this division was two years ago

81

before he took over . . .' And then I will spend a minute or two recounting his glorious achievements. There are two benefits to this. Joe doesn't waste twenty minutes congratulating himself *and* it puts him in a far better light because I said it.

Of course, you can always take the executive aside before the meeting and tell him what not to say. But this private meeting is only a 50% solution: you've stopped his self-serving statement, but you've missed a chance to praise him.

After all, there is a big difference between telling someone privately that they are doing a fine job and saying so in front of his peers. Meetings are excellent places to hand out compliments. The bigger the audience the better.

3. Confrontations

Casey Stengel said, 'The secret to managing a baseball club is to keep the five people who hate you from talking to the five people who are undecided.'

I think that applies to confrontations in meetings.

If I'm running a meeting, I try to anticipate the confrontational items. I know which subjects are inflammatory and where most of the people in the room stand on the issues. I also know that heated arguments in a meeting tend to be very dispiriting affairs. They rarely shed light on the subject and they trouble everyone but the combatants.

If I want certain subjects to go unmentioned, I will tell the key people beforehand, 'I know how you feel about this problem, but I really don't want to get into that discussion today.' I'll gladly admit to overcontrolling if the payoff is a smoother meeting with fewer hostilities and more people making a contribution.

On the other hand, I try just as hard not to go over the line and completely stifle debate. If confrontations can bog down a meeting, then their complete absence can make a meeting pointless.

No matter how powerful or wise you think you are, you have to fight the all-too-common compulsion to use the meeting to wrap up an issue and decide it your way.

In my experience, meetings don't work that way. Issues are rarely decided on the spot after you've heard oral arguments. The decision usually comes days or weeks later, after you've had time to think about it. The key, however, is to let everyone be heard. Here is a maxim I admire:

'It is better to debate an issue without settling it than to settle an issue without debating it.'

4. The bigger the meeting the smaller the return

The funny thing about meetings is that, no matter how much people complain about them, nobody wants to be excluded from one that everyone else is attending. Meetings become status symbols. People fight to be included. As a result, many meetings outgrow their optimum size.

There is no perfect size for a meeting. But if you have thirty people in a room listening to three people discussing the minutiae of a topic, that is not an efficient meeting.

Every discussion in a meeting has a diminishing curve of interest. The longer the discussion goes on, the fewer people will be interested in it.

For example, if we start off a tennis division meeting by talking about revenue growth and new clients, that's interesting to everyone. When we move on to a discussion of the international television market for tennis, that too has some educational value to everyone.

But let's say we move on to the subject of how we plan the Italian Open. Ideally, only five people need to be involved in that discussion: the head of our Italian office, the person responsible for foreign television sales, the head of the tennis division and the two agents of the clients we want to play there.

The television executive says he can't sell the Australian TV rights to the tournament unless a quality field is playing.

'What's a quality field?' asks our Italian chief.

'Three of the top five players.'

'That's too expensive. What if we only have two players?'

83

'Then the TV fee goes down.'

What you have is a discussion among five people, with everyone else in the room reduced to listening. Some of what they hear is educational; it's good for our people to see how we plan a tournament.

But as the conversation continues, the returns diminish for almost everyone in the room. This applies to almost every item brought up in a meeting. You start off holding everyone's interest, but as you delve into specifics you have fewer and fewer people involved – and even fewer paying attention.

Be alert to this. Keep your meetings going forward. It can be tough, but learn to say 'Move along'.

It is more interesting to explore a topic than to exhaust it.

If people need to know more about a subject, tell them they can discuss it later – in a different setting.

How to Stone Goliath

There are plenty of moments in life when we feel we are at a competitive disadvantage. We haven't as much money or talent or experience as the other fellow. We feel like an amateur playing against a pro.

This is the feeling I used to get when I went cap in hand to large corporations to convince them to spend some of their marketing budgets on sports.

The whole process was designed to intimidate me.

First, it would take me weeks or months to get through to the top decision-maker.

Then I would call on the executive at his headquarters – where the intimidation not only continued but intensified.

My humble four-person office in Cleveland couldn't compare to this giant's edifice.

His corridors were longer.

His office was larger.

His chairs were plusher.

His mahogany conference table was shinier.

His paintings were costlier.

His china service was finer.

His entourage was bigger.

Even his secretaries were quieter.

And there I sat. Alone. Clutching my briefcase. Proposing that he should give a little more thought to the game of golf.

It would be nice to report that I walked away from those first sales calls with major contracts for our clients. That would provide a fairy-tale ending for these face-offs between David (me) and Goliath. Alas, that wouldn't be true.

But in defeat, I gradually learned an important thing about corporate titans. Despite the power plays and intimidation ploys – one CEO had his desk built on a raised platform so that I had to look up to him; another sat with blinding sunlight behind him, making it impossible to read his face – they are just human beings. They wanted to look good and be liked – just like me. If I could concentrate my sales pitch on this human level, then the fine china, plush chairs and expensive art wouldn't matter. We would be on an equal footing.

Realizing the opposition is human is hardly a profundity. But it is if you are a little guy who is scared silly.

Here are other, not-so-obvious words of wisdom when facing Goliaths:

Hierarchy is man-made

When I first dealt with John DeLorean, who ran the Pontiac division of General Motors in the 1960s and '70s, I could see that he was a maverick who wanted to do his own deals, even in the relatively small area of sports marketing.

What happened in the wake of my meetings with DeLorean, however, was astonishing. For some reason, I began to be perceived as someone who had the boss's ear. Pontiac executives would approach me and try to glean what DeLorean had been saying about them. Executives at Pontiac's advertising agency

85

would want to meet with me to urge DeLorean to continue to use them.

I remember being present once when DeLorean visited his Detroit agency. This apparently was unprecedented. A General Motors division chief didn't make 'house calls' on his advertising agency. The world came to him. I was astonished to see ostensibly hard-boiled and sophisticated executives unravel at the prospect of his visit. 'DeLorean is coming,' they kept saying. 'Why? What does he want? What did we do wrong?'

Even more baffling, DeLorean was coming alone. No entourage, no assistants, no toadies, no bean counters. This was beyond the advertising executives' comprehension.

Once you grasp how insecure people in the chain of command really are, corporate hierarchies aren't so intimidating.

Find the weak link

Every organization or group, no matter how stiff or proper it seems, contains a maverick, a wild card, someone who takes pleasure at flouting the rules or flaunting his independence.

They are your opening. They are the weak link in the chain of command. They can help you triumph over bureaucracy, because they are masters at fighting it themselves. The fact that your company is small or that you have an unconventional idea won't matter. With mavericks, it is probably an advantage.

Quite often, you'll find, the mavericks are at the top of the organization.

I remember one chairman of a major sports event who was a genuine visionary. He was always battling with his conservative board of directors to bring the event into the twentieth century. It didn't take me long to figure out that if I had even a remotely daring concept, I should take it to him rather than to his directors. If he liked it, he would then steer me step by step through his various committees so that my concept could win approval.

Years later, when he had retired as chairman, we still kept in touch. He continued to counsel me on how to convince the board of directors. Ever the maverick, he loved tweaking the chain of command even when he was a missing link.

Mavericks, by the way, can be found in any organization, whether it is a company or your local government or a community volunteer group. Who is the official or deputy mayor who returns your calls? Who sounds interested in your concept? Who has a similar background or education? Who lives in your neighbourhood? Whose children go to the same school as yours? Who shares your taste in movies, sports, books, music, food or fashion?

Find a kindred spirit in the chain of command, and you can bring the most gigantic and daunting bureaucracies down to your size.

Rank gravitates towards equal rank

Most organizations have a pecking order. Chairmen prefer to talk to chairmen. CEOs talk to other CEOs. Senior vice-presidents deal with their vice-presidential counterparts at other companies. Secretaries talk to secretaries.

What is interesting about this, even at the chairman's level, is that it doesn't really matter what you are chairman of.

The chairman of General Motors regards the chairman of Rolex as an equal, even though billions in revenues separate one from the other.

I recognized this happening in our organization. Over the years I gained access to CEOs of companies that were a hundred times IMG's size – because I was a CEO. Likewise our senior executives deal as equals with division chiefs responsible for thousands of employees and huge revenues.

One of our sales executives once offered to forgo an increase in compensation if we would upgrade his title. The more impressive business card, he reasoned, would give him so much credibility with decision-makers that he would make up for the lost salary within a year.

Information is the great equalizer

Once you get a seat at the table with the big guys, you have to be able to hold your own. As a small operator, your most important asset is information and you probably know more than you think you do. Don't take information particular to you for granted and don't underestimate how interesting a top executive or large organization might find it.

Contrary to popular opinion, the chairmen and CEOs of big companies are not omnipotent or omniscient. They tend to be generalists. But they are omnivorous when it comes to information. In fact, you'll find that the higher you go in the chain of command, the more hungry the players are for apparently arcane news.

Not long ago I met with Yoshiaki Tsutsumi, who controls Japan's Seibu Railway and has extensive hotel and resort holdings there. He is perhaps the world's richest man, a very significant presence in his country's business life and a great supporter of the Olympic movement.

During our talk, he asked me what I thought could be done to improve his hotels.

'You should serve brewed decaffeinated coffee,' I said. I pointed out that in America, if you have ten people ordering coffee at a dinner table, at least half will want decaf. Yet in Japan's most elegant hotels, if you order decaf, all you get is a pot of hot water, a container of crystals – and terrible coffee.

Tsutsumi turned to his translator and said, '*This* is precisely the kind of information I need.'

That's typical of people at the top. Like many others, Tsutsumi is insulated by layers and layers of bureaucracy. His people want to 'protect' him from bad news. They tell him only what they think he wants to hear. Yet he is brilliant and curious and absolutely determined to smash through these barriers. He was conducting consumer research, and I was the consumer.

Sometimes the people at the top have very idiosyncratic uses for your information. When David Foster was the chairman of

Colgate-Palmolive, I could tell that he would personally oversee every aspect of his company's involvement in sports. He loved upstaging his advertising agency with all the inside information and marketing ideas. So I made a major effort to feed Foster the information he craved.

In sum, no matter how small you are, you can play on the same field as giants.

The 110% Partner

If you want to maximize your performance at anything, hook up with someone who is better than you. Nothing will force you to give 110% more than having to keep up with someone who is already giving that much.

You see this dynamic at work all the time in sports. A great player joins a floundering team and immediately team-mates rise towards his level. Larry Bird did this in 1979 with the Boston Celtics. Within a year the Celtics improved their record from 29 wins and 53 losses to 61 and 21. It remains the greatest single season turnaround in professional basketball history – and you can't credit it to the mere addition of Larry Bird's own performance.

Perhaps the most obvious 'partner effect' occurs in tennis doubles. Middling players such as Ken Flach and Robert Seguso somehow enhance each other's abilities when they team up. Neither ever ranked higher than No. 20 in the world in singles, but they were the pair to beat in the late 1980s. Their sum was greater than their parts.

The doubles team of John McEnroe and Peter Fleming, which won four Wimbledon and three US Open titles in the late 1970s and early '80s, is equally instructive. McEnroe was already a supremely talented player; Fleming was a mere mortal. But through some athletic alchemy McEnroe helped Fleming become better than he had any right to be. Peter Fleming always served better, moved faster, hit more confident strokes and displayed more disdain for his opponents with John McEnroe beside him than he ever did playing singles.

You can see this even in a game as individualistic as golf. You usually don't think of golf as a team sport. Basically, it's you alone against the course. Yet I've seen executives and amateurs play way over their heads when they teamed up for a round with Arnold Palmer. Arnold's will to win is infectious, even among people he has known only for a few hours. When people play on his team, they are more focused, more alert and, I suspect, scared to death of disappointing him.

You see the same thing happen on the professional circuit. The championship golfer Dave Marr once told me that he always tried to play the practice rounds before a tournament with the top money-winners. It was the best way to find out what they were doing right and give his own game an instant boost.

As Marr puts it: 'Great players raise the level of your game. When you play with a Nicklaus, Palmer, Hogan, Snead or Trevino, you're sharper. You want to beat them. That's why you see so many so-called upsets in sports. The great players literally force their lesser opponents to play beyond their capacities.'

Marr rates his favourite experience in golf, even more memorable than winning the PGA Championship in 1965, as the Easter Sunday of 1964 when he played the final round with Palmer at Augusta when Arnold won his fourth Masters.

'The whole day is frozen in time for me,' Marr says. 'I remember every shot that Arnold and I hit. It was one of those moments when I overachieved and got a little more out of myself. The gallery was huge. It was my first national exposure on television. I was playing way over my head, thinking I could win, and having a great time with Arnold.

'At one point, Arnold three-putted the tenth hole and I pulled within three strokes. I was really wired and charged toward the eleventh tee. Somewhere behind me I overheard Ironman, Arnold's caddy, ask him, "Boss, are you choking?" I burst out laughing. It was such an outrageous thing to say. But it was a pretty grim moment for Arnold. Of course, he overcame that. He bore down and took control of the tournament.

'He was a gentleman to play with. On the eighteenth tee, when he was leading by six strokes and I needed a birdie to tie Jack Nicklaus for second, he asked if there was anything he could do to help. All I could say was, "Yeah, shoot 12". But it loosened me up and I birdied the hole.'

Sometimes linking up with a new partner can improve your performance, even when most people think you are already at the top of your game. Pat Summerall, the CBS sports broadcaster, says that is what happened to him when he teamed up with our client John Madden to announce National Football League games.

By any criterion, Summerall is one of the best in the business. A former professional football player, he has been at CBS for thirty years. He is knowledgeable, unflappable and blessed with a great voice. When Americans tune in CBS to watch some of the most prestigious events in sports – the US Open tennis championships, the Masters golf tournament, the National Football League playoffs or the Super Bowl – the man describing the action is Summerall.

He is most visible during the football season. For years his partner in the broadcast booth was Tom Brookshier, like Summerall a former National Football League star. Summerall handled the play-by-play chores, Brookshier analysed the action. They were the network's A team, assigned to the most important game each week. Summerall took tremendous pride in that fact. He thought the partnership could go on forever.

But in 1981 CBS broke up the combination and paired Summerall with a new football analyst, John Madden.

Madden is something of a media phenomenon now, with three best-selling books, his TV commercials and a nationally syndicated radio programme. Back then, however, he was just another former football coach (albeit a tremendously successful one with the Oakland Raiders) who had made the move to broadcasting. He was untested and unproven on television. But he had a blunt, funny, rough-diamond quality

91

that viewers seemed to like. And he knew a lot about football.

To appreciate the effect Madden had on Summerall, it is important to know a little about what it takes to broadcast a football game. 'Before Madden,' as Summerall likes to say, 'it was a social event. You had dinner with the production staff on Friday night. On Saturday you met with the teams' public relations people, maybe talked to some of the players, maybe not. We arrived laughing and left laughing.'

Madden changed that. He prepared for each game with the dedication of a head coach. He showed up two or three days before the game and insisted on interviewing the assistant coaches, trainers and equipment managers as well as the 'usual suspects'. He mingled with the players on the practice field, searching for clues about who was strong and who was hurting. And he spent hours looking at film.

'Of all the people I've known in broadcasting,' Summerall says, 'John Madden is the hardest worker and the most conscientious. If you're supposed to be there at 9.15, he's there at 9 a.m. If you're ready to do two hours, he's ready to do four. If he's interviewing someone, he will not leave the scene until he gets a usable answer. The rest of us are thinking, "Let's go to dinner", and he's saying, "Let's do it again". If you're watching film, he'll run it back twenty times until he sees why the play broke down.

'John makes everyone around him – the producer, the director, the cameraman – better. They all try harder.

'I realized that working with him I would have to be on my toes or he would leave me in the dust. I always enjoyed the game but I was at arm's length for a while. He actually made me a fan again.'

The effort shows on the TV screen. Summerall and Madden are the standard against which other football broadcasters now are measured. They cover the most important games and make the game itself more important.

Madden, for his part, knows precisely how *his* partner helps him. 'Pat is my safety net on *all* aspects of broadcasting,' he says.

'I know a lot about football and zero about broadcasting. Pat knows a lot of both because he was a great player and has been a great broadcaster for so long.

'He's seen it all. Whenever there's a problem, I step aside and let him handle it. The audience doesn't notice this, but I do. There has never been a time when he has complained or criticized me, and I'm sure he's had to live through some grating moments. He just takes over and lets me concentrate on football.'

Unfortunately, not all of us get to work with talented people who complement our abilities or inspire us to exceed them.

Finding the 110% partner – whether competitor, client or spouse – is a stroke of luck. And the most important aspect of that luck is knowing when you've been lucky.

As in most things in life, however, you help make your own luck. Like Dave Marr intentionally playing practice rounds with winners rather than losers, you too can choose your 'partners' with greater care.

I think we are born with this instinct but unfortunately lose it over time. As schoolkids we certainly have it when we pick the strongest player for our side in a playground game. We know that the best player not only improves our chances of winning, but the best player is also more likely to catch our passes or get the ball to us when we're in a position to score. The best player makes us better.

But we seem to lose this partnering instinct as we get older, as we become more aware that our performance is being judged and compared against others. Suddenly, our sense of self-interest makes us seek weaker partners, who make us look stronger by comparison, rather than the 110% partner who can elevate our performance.

We lose this valuable instinct bit by bit. We lose it as college students when we choose teachers who grade easily rather than seek out the best and most demanding professors. We lose it when we choose courses we know we can pass. We lose it as employees when we form alliances with mediocre bosses who

93

won't demand as much from us or mediocre peers who may be easier to dominate or outshine.

So the next time you fall short of a goal or feel you're not living up to your expectations, take a look at the partners you've chosen. Perhaps you've been too easy on yourself.

The 110% Opponent

Sometimes the 110% partner will appear in the form of a worthy opponent.

Bjorn Borg, for example, elevated the game of an entire generation of tennis players. He hit the ball with such overpowering topspin that his opponents had to enhance their repertoire simply to stay on the court with him. Those who insisted on sticking with their game soon fell off the tour. The smart ones, willing to learn from Borg and challenge him with topspin of their own, ultimately improved their performance – and occasionally beat him.

The same kind of thing happened in one of our company's first forays into television. MCA, the media conglomerate that owns Universal Pictures, wanted to produce a series of televised 'golf challenges' using our clients. Being novices in TV, we didn't know what a programme cost or how it was produced. We didn't know how to write a contract or what points to demand on behalf of our clients.

Our counterparts at MCA were experts at this and, quite frankly, we were intimidated by them. They had years of experience in dealing with stars, budgets, production schedules and TV contracts.

At some point we realized that dealing with such a formidable opponent could actually be to our advantage – if we were willing to acknowledge the opponent's strength.

Since we trusted MCA, why not let it draft the contract? Their lawyers' boilerplate text was probably better than our best effort. They knew the key points. They knew the troublesome clauses. They might highlight or concede points that we would never have considered. We let MCA show us how to write a state-of-the-art television contract, one that has served as our model for three decades.

That's the beauty of the 110% opponent. Change your perspective slightly and he may become a 110% partner.

CHAPTER SIX

How to Make Your Career

If you could put a clock on it, I'd bet that people spend more time thinking about their boss than about any other business relationship. After all, the boss is *the* individual who can make or break your career. A boss can create an atmosphere that is friendly or paranoid, efficient or muddled.

It is ironic that with so much brainpower devoted to reading the boss's mind and divining his or her moods, people still manage to get the relationship wrong. Instead of making their careers, their relationship with the boss ends up breaking them.

Most of us know the basics of being among the bossed:

Be loyal

Bosses will forgive carelessness, stupidity, tardiness and the occasional temper tantrum. These can be corrected, but disloyalty is a true character flaw. You cannot – and will not – be trusted.

Keep the boss informed

Such as about what you are doing, where you are, who you are talking to and why. If you must err, err on the side of overkill. Bombard the boss with bulletins, memos and FYIs until he says, 'Stop!' No one has ever lost his job for telling the boss too much.

Embrace change, even if you do not understand it

Any boss must, as part of his job, instigate change. It is not your job to resist.

Respect the boss's time

If you need thirty minutes with him, don't take sixty. Better yet, take twenty.

Don't tread on his turf

Or at least not without permission.

Follow up quickly

Bosses don't pull out a stopwatch when they give a command. But, believe me, their internal clock is ticking.

These principles will serve you well, whether your boss is a genius or a jerk. Follow them and you will never fall behind your peers. You will always be regarded as someone who is attentive, responsive and true. But in time, you may need some different strategies to break away from the pack. Consider the following:

Look for the veiled command

Like most people, you probably have the good sense to obey a direct command. If the boss says 'Jump', you jump. But the best bosses are not so crude. They want subordinates to think for themselves and, therefore, they don't give explicit orders. They *imply*. Be alert to this.

One tactic you can't afford to ignore is the veiled command –

when the boss suggests a course of action but says the decision is up to you.

The veiled command comes in many forms but it is usually a variation on, 'I think you should pursue this project, but you decide.' The problem with this implied command is that it is ambiguous to everyone but the boss. And the danger, of course, is that subordinates hear only what they want to hear – the wrong half of the message.

This happened not long ago to a man at a company with which we have a consulting arrangement. Our contract was expiring, but senior management there assured us it would be renewed. As I understand it, the young man, who had been our contact at the company, was told by his boss, 'We think that IMG's contract should be renewed, but it is your call.'

As often happens in consulting arrangements where we are paid to teach staffers what we know, this young man believed he had learned all he could. He heard his boss say 'It's your call' and acted accordingly by delaying our renewal. He ignored the veiled command in the more important half of the message. We still have a consulting contract. And the man is no longer on our account.

Don't bet the ranch on one boss

Each of us knows employees who take advantage of their proximity or access to the head of their company. Having a mentor or ally in the top ranks can give your career a powerful boost. But betting your career on the boss is a double-edged sword. Your fortunes can change dramatically should your boss alter his opinion of you or himself stumble or disappear.

A few years ago, an entrepreneur I know sold his company to a large conglomerate. He stayed on to run the business, reporting directly to the conglomerate's chairman. The arrangement flourished for the next three years. Then the chairman retired. Within months, the entrepreneur resigned.

When I asked him about it, he said, 'The mistake I made was dealing exclusively with the chairman. It was great while it lasted.

No interference, no bureaucracy. But I ignored the layer of senior vice-presidents. When the chairman left, I had no one in senior management who either knew me or cared enough to support my ideas. Perhaps they were gunning for me, but I got out before things got ugly.'

Use the boss

Bosses like to be used, no matter how isolated they seem or how far removed they are from day-to-day activities. Every boss loves to be given an opportunity to demonstrate that he or she can still hack it in the trenches.

I am constantly exhorting people in our company to use me – to open a door, make an introduction, smooth out a crisis, speed a transaction or simply to verify a fact. And every once in a while, a smart executive takes me up on the offer.

Recently one of our top tennis players received a ludicrously high offer to appear in a series of exhibitions overseas. The offer was so high that the player's agent grew suspicious. This happens sometimes. A promoter will float a big number to get our superstar's commitment and then use that commitment to line up the financing and the rest of the field. In the meantime, our client locks that time period into his schedule with no guarantee that the event will come off as planned.

It is our job to separate the bogus offers from the genuine. In this case, the detective work would have taken weeks. Our executive asked if I could help. With a single call, I was able to determine that the offer was a fake. The next day I called the player and told him to stay at home.

I found out later that the player was flabbergasted not only at how fast we worked but that I was willing to get involved.

A minor episode, perhaps, but in my book 110% effective – because the results far outweighed the effort of one phone call.

Don't be afraid to use the boss to achieve your objectives. If you do it right, you will get ahead – and make your boss's day.

When You Ride on Somebody's Coat-tails, Make Sure He Is in the Suit

Name-dropping is not the world's most attractive social strategem. But there are times when it is useful.

The fact is, a great many of our social and professional successes, perhaps more than we care to admit, are dependent on our ability to drop the right names.

If we want to join a private club, the application process seems to demand that we list a socially prominent name as our sponsor. When we apply to schools or enter the workforce we face the same need. The careful deployment of an influential name as a reference often influences the decision more than our qualifications.

This may not be fair, but it is the way of the world. Most of us are willing to bend things in our favour if all that is required is the relatively harmless act of mentioning that we know someone consequential.

Note, however, that I am not endorsing name-dropping in its more insidious form – that is, the naked display of whom you know simply as a means of displaying self-importance. That tactic rarely impresses people; more likely, it has the opposite effect.

Nowhere is name-dropping a more revered tactic than in sales, where getting your foot in the door is the most important – and often the most difficult – objective.

In the sports business we know that representing well-known clients and being able to propose concepts with some glamour and sizzle attached to them is one of the biggest advantages we have. We'd be foolish not to use it.

Thus, if we're having trouble persuading a potential customer to take our call, we might say that we are calling on behalf of a famous athlete or, better yet, we'll have the athlete actually place the call. Without fail, the other party snaps to attention, if only out of curiosity to find out why a superstar is on the line. And then it is up to us to keep the ball rolling.

Because many of our company's relationships began with me,

I also encourage our people to use my name, if necessary, in reaching top executives whom I may know. The judicious use of 'Mr McCormack suggested I call you' carries some weight in our business.

I'm sure the same could be said of the boss's name at almost any company.

The only thing to remember when dropping names to open doors is to keep everyone informed of how you are using their name. Otherwise the results can be embarrassing, as the following incident shows.

A few years ago our client Bjorn Borg was having all-day business meetings in our New York office with some of our executives to discuss a new venture he was forming. Also present was a gentleman Bjorn had hired to run his new company (we'll call him the President).

The meetings went well and at the last minute the President decided to invite everyone to dinner that evening to Bice, an extremely popular midtown Italian restaurant. Using Bjorn Borg's name, he reserved a table for eight people for seven o'clock.

The *maître d'* at Bice was delighted. 'We look forward to seeing Mr Borg and his party at seven,' he said.

Unfortunately, the meeting didn't end until eight o'clock, at which point everyone went their separate ways, agreeing to meet in thirty minutes at Bice. The President prudently called the restaurant to say Mr Borg's party would be late.

'No problem,' said the *maître d'*. 'Mr Borg's table is yours for the night. Come when you can.'

At 8.30 seven of the eight people – but not Bjorn – arrived at Bice and were ushered through the crowded waiting room to the best table in the house. They ordered a round of drinks and told the *maître d'* that they would wait for Bjorn before ordering.

'Do not worry. The kitchen is at Mr Borg's disposal,' he replied.

A half-hour passed. More drinks. More lively conversation. But no Bjorn Borg.

The President called over the *maître d'* and said, 'We'd like to see the menu.'

The *maître d'* replied, 'Perhaps we should wait a few more minutes for Mr Borg.' And he walked away.

A slight chill descended over the table. One of the executives was dispatched to call Bjorn's hotel only to return a few minutes later with the not totally surprising news that Bjorn was tired, had ordered room service and was calling it a night. Borg often would decide to do that.

The President again hailed the *maître d'* and asked for menus. Again the *maître d'* assured him that there was no need to hurry, that they would wait for Mr Borg, and disappeared.

At this point, one of our executives leaned over to the President and explained what was apparent to everyone. 'The *maître d'* is angry,' he said. 'He's seen people make reservations in the name of celebrities many times, and then the celebrity doesn't show. He is not going to serve us unless Bjorn Borg appears.

'You have two options. First, you can walk over there and explain to him who we are, what's happened to Bjorn and how you are quite embarrassed by this turn of events. Tell him that you fully appreciate the effort he has made on our behalf and his disappointment. Then give him $50 for his trouble and we'll probably get the chance to eat.

'Or you can take the view that your patronage is just as important as that of Bjorn Borg, in which case we'll sit here, we'll be ignored and a year from now we'll talk about this as a memorable evening indeed.'

The President, to his credit, apologized to the *maître d'*, tipped him well and the dinner proceeded without interruption.

The lesson is clear: if you're going to ride on somebody's coat-tails, make sure he is in the suit.

Take My Advice, Please

You're never more vulnerable than at those moments when you need advice – when you realize you don't fully comprehend a situation and have to rely on someone else's judgement.

But you also are never more in control: you are the one who decides who to turn to, how well to listen and how seriously to act on their counsel.

Some people aren't good at taking advice. They can't admit they need help. They can't accept that someone may know more than they do. They ask the wrong questions. They can't deal with conflicting advice. They only hear what they want to hear or what confirms their own opinion. They listen to the wrong people. Or to too many people. And even if they choose the right advisers, they misinterpret the advice, or don't believe it or only follow half of it.

Some people don't think that taking advice is important. To them it is a sign of weakness rather than a necessary social skill. It is passive rather than active. No one congratulates you for being good at it. (When was the last time someone praised you for 'taking advice well'?) In the advice game, we all would rather be perceived as the one dispensing wisdom rather than seeking it.

Here are four steps to getting good advice:

1. Admit you need it

This is a humbling procedure, but it means you're on the right track. It means you've identified a problem and are prepared to correct it. It also means you're prepared to listen.

2. Consider the source

Your best sources of advice are people who have no axe to grind and nothing to gain by offering you their counsel. You don't have to worry about hidden agendas and ulterior motives with these advisers. You don't have to ask, 'Why is this person telling me this?'

Finding a disinterested party is often the most difficult part of getting advice. People tend to look in all the wrong places. When they have a problem, they turn to the nearest available source rather than the best one. They seek out their friends, their peers,

103

their parents or their spouse. There is nothing wrong with this sometimes. But if you really need a disinterested party, the chances are that you won't find it close to home.

For example, if you're a mother and housewife thinking about returning to the workforce, who do you turn to? Your husband? He might support the idea because the second income is appealing. Or he might fight it because he wants someone at home taking care of the children, the house and the meals.

Your best friend next door? She might argue against it because she is jealous or doesn't want to lose a helpful neighbour.

Neither can be considered a disinterested party. And yet they might be the first people you would allow to advise you.

Parents are also dangerous advisers, not because they don't mean well (they always do) but rather because they inject personal considerations into areas that call for objectivity. If you are offered a job half-way around the world, your parents might take a position against it based solely on the fear that they will never see you and your children. Their advice may be logical, loving and sound, but it is not necessarily given with your best professional interests at heart.

The same thing happens at work. If the people closest to you in your personal life are not always 100% disinterested, you can be sure that your associates in the workplace are less so. There are not enough pages in this book to chronicle the multiplicity of interests and cross-purposes that come into play when we ask a colleague for professional advice. You would have to be incredibly naive and trusting not to be aware of this.

In our company, for example, I'm convinced that on certain matters advice from our executives is virtually useless.

If I sought their advice on where the San Francisco office should fit in our reporting structure, I wouldn't be surprised if a half dozen of them responded, 'The San Francisco office should report to me.' Their reasons would differ – some would want the bigger power base, others might simply be angling for an excuse to visit San Francisco more often – but they're each grinding an axe.

On this matter, and others, I'm better off getting advice not so close to home.

3. Go to the right source

Christie Hefner, the chief executive of Playboy, has all the usual attributes of a successful CEO – she is brainy, decisive and knows how to delegate – but she is an absolute champion at getting good advice.

As Hugh Hefner's daughter, she is viewed as the lucky woman who 'inherited' the Playboy empire. In actual fact, what Christie found in 1982 was a company in chaos. Playboy was bleeding $50 million a year, it had lost its profitable casino business and its flagship magazine seemed out of step with the times.

Through hard work and shrewd management, Hefner cut the losses, rebuilt the core businesses and turned the company around. The truth is, she wasn't lucky to get control of Playboy; Playboy was lucky to get her.

Unlike many people who feel compelled to prove that they can think and act on their own, the moment she took over Playboy Hefner made a conscious effort to build a powerful network of advisers. As she puts it, 'You can never have too many smart people in your life.'

She immediately formed an Office of the President so that she could take advantage of a very strong financial executive whose advice she couldn't afford to lose. A less secure person might have forced him out.

In forming her board of directors, she intentionally left off paid advisers, such as her investment banker, her lawyer and her auditor, because she already had them as resources. Nor did she bring a lot of insiders on to the board because she was already tapping into their talent at work. Again, a less secure person might have stacked the board with consultants and yes-men, their allegiance already bought and paid for. Christie's method, in contrast, essentially multiplied her pool of advisers.

She sought out people whose interests, at first glance, seemed at odds with Playboy's image.

Consider how she met Warren Buffett, the legendary investor from Omaha, Nebraska. The approach illustrates her method of getting good advice: (1) identify the problem, (2) find an expert who can help and (3) don't be shy about asking him or her.

Hefner was aware of the amazing track record Buffett had as chairman of Berkshire Hathaway. He was an acknowledged master at spotting valuable franchises and developing those assets over the long term.

Christie wrote to Buffett. She pointed out that she, too, was intent on building long-term value at a company with an established franchise. She offered to buy him lunch if he was ever in Chicago, New York or Los Angeles.

Buffett wrote back within the week, explaining that he was rarely in those cities, but he'd be happy to see her if she ever passed through Omaha. He also mentioned that he would be spending New Year's weekend with his family on the California coast just north of San Diego and that she was welcome to stop by if she was in the neighbourhood. Christie made a point of being in the neighbourhood and spent an enlightening afternoon with Buffett. Since then, she has called on him a couple of times in Omaha.

One letter. One visit. One valuable adviser.

If you need good advice, don't expect it to fall out of the sky. Seek it out – conscientiously, consistently and aggressively.

4. Build a board of advisers

For the last fifteen years, I have maintained an informal board of advisers at our company – several extremely successful business people, many of whom started out as my customers and all of whom are now my friends.

I turned to this arrangement about the time when our growth had outpaced our internal management structure. We had achieved our objectives and were in that perilous grey area between being a small company and becoming a much larger one.

I realized that I didn't have the infrastructure to manage this transition, so I sought outsiders who had experience of running large companies. I was totally open with them, giving them access to our most intimate details so they would be candid with me about how we ran our company.

I didn't expect them to teach me about managing athletes or sports marketing. I didn't need them to teach me *my* business. I needed them to advise me on the fundamentals of running *any* business. One, for example, is very savvy about corporate structures and employee compensation. Another is an expert at banking and finance. Still another knows more about the media than I will ever know.

For me, this advisory group is a major improvement on the standard use of paid consultants, who are often more interested in retaining you as a client than in solving your problems. Since my advisers have careers independent of me, they can afford to talk to me bluntly. And unlike many consultants who infiltrate a company and then proceed to threaten or irritate the employees, these advisers don't interfere in our operations. Their only brief is to educate me in areas where I need to be smarter.

The logistics are simple. I meet with one or more of them on an as-needed basis. There is no bylaw requiring the entire group to convene. And I try to have at least one of them present at all important meetings.

The benefits are simple, too. They are compensated, they get to use their expertise in new areas and they get the satisfaction of helping a friend. I see no reason why this arrangement couldn't work in any individual's life.

An attorney told me once that in preparing wills for his clients he always felt a tinge of sorrow when they asked him to be the executor of their estate. 'If I was the only person they could ask,' he said, 'that told me they had failed to build a solid support system in their life. There's something sad about people who feel they cannot rely on the judgement of their friends. The sad part is that they probably could rely on their friends, but they never bothered to ask.'

I've always been puzzled by people who are defensive about

107

needing advice, or feel that they are imposing on a friend by telling them their troubles.

On the contrary, turning to people for counsel – whether they are a doctor, clergyman, lawyer, accountant, mechanic, fitness instructor or hairdresser – is the highest compliment you can pay them. It indicates that you respect them, trust them and think they are wise.

My advice: *Do it more often*.

Your First Impression Doesn't Matter as Much as Your Last One

We're all familiar with the cliché, 'You don't get a second chance to make a first impression.' Most of us believe it. I don't.

First impressions are overrated. The impression that really matters is the last one; it supports or negates all the others you've made.

The chronically late among us make an extra effort to be on time for a first meeting with someone important whether that someone is a major sales prospect, our company's CEO or our child's schoolteacher.

Even people who don't put much stock in their physical appearance haul out a new suit or dress before an important job interview or first date. It's a simple drill. We all know it and practise it.

Having made the effort to impress someone by being on time and dressing well, we then assume that we have achieved the desired effect. So we relax. We are not as punctual or attentive to our appearance the next time. And even less so at the third meeting.

That is one reason you hear people say, 'I can't be late for my first meeting with Mr Smith.' And yet they rarely ever think to themselves, 'I can't be late for my *fourteenth* meeting with Mr Smith.'

Some people are superb at first impressions. They dress well, show up on time, have a firm handshake, look you in the eye, know all the right buzzwords and latest jokes. But if they come back a second time with the same routine – the same banter and smile – we may sense they lack substance.

Bud Stanner, now the head of our North American marketing group, has a story about his first three meetings with me. At each, Stanner learned something new about me or our company.

Meeting Number One: Stanner was a vice-president at Head Skis and eager to sign a contract with our client, Jean-Claude Killy. He flew to Cleveland to talk to me. It was late, so I sent a car to pick him up at the airport and bring him to my home. I introduced him to my family and we talked for twenty minutes in my study. Afterwards, the driver took him to his hotel.

Meeting Number Two: Stanner happened to be in our Cleveland office a few weeks later. I had arrived on a red-eye from the West Coast and Stanner stopped by to say hello. Bud made some polite small talk about how I must be tired after flying all night, to which I rather snappishly responded, 'Well, I'm not tired!'

Meeting Number Three: This wasn't actually a meeting. It was a courtesy call after we had concluded a Head–Killy agreement. I phoned Stanner at his hotel in Denver to tell him that I thought the Killy contract was important, that I hoped the relationship would last for years and that he should feel free to call me at any time.

Unbeknown to me, each of these encounters affected Stanner in a different way.

Dispatching a car sent a clear message that even though we were a small company, we were a classy one and a big organization such as Head should be aware of that.

Protesting that I wasn't tired gave the impression that I worked very hard at a high energy level.

Phoning him to tell him I was never too busy to take his calls made *him* feel important.

Three encounters. Three different snapshots of me. I cannot claim that I thought all this out beforehand. In fact, I don't remember these occasions with the same clarity as Stanner.

But through the years I've come to realize that *it is the small things, not the big deals, that build an enduring relationship.*

Think about the long-term relationships in your life, in or out of the workplace. The chances are that they didn't blossom because someone overwhelmed you the first time you met, but rather because they continued to influence you on the second, third and fourth occasions. The most solid relationships are comprised of a series of impressions that reinforce and build on one another.

Nowadays, whenever I meet someone, I'm extremely conscious of the initial impression I want to make. And I make a point of not only remembering that but factoring it into the future impressions I need to make.

A good first impression, by the way, does not have to be an ingratiating one. Sometimes you are actually better off antagonizing the other party.

A few years ago our company met roadblocks in dealing with a Japanese media conglomerate. The chairman was a strong-willed individual who could not abide agents and middlemen, which is exactly what we were. That feeling permeated his company and made it difficult for us to do business. In bidding for the television rights to sports properties we represented, his executives were constantly trying end-runs and coming up empty-handed.

A meeting was arranged between the chairman and myself to hammer out something of a truce. He arrived at our New York office, trailed by the entourage of yes-men that sometimes travel with Japanese tycoons.

Choosing my words carefully, I said, 'You have not dealt with us in a proper or ethical way. You should have pursued these properties through us. If you had, the result would have been different and more favourable to you.'

The chairman was taken aback by this bluntness. He said that people did not talk to him that way often. He was right: I didn't care and I wanted him to know that. As we parted, he said that he would review the situation when he returned to Japan.

(*First impression:* McCormack is tough.)

In our second meeting the chairman appeared chastened. He was interested in the TV rights to a golf property that we did not represent, and he was caught in a tough bidding contest with Japanese competitors. He was ready to listen to us. He needed advice.

Having told him in our first meeting that if he played by my rules, he would be more successful, it was my turn to put up or shut up. So we outlined a bidding strategy. He followed the strategy and he won.

(*Second impression:* McCormack is not only tough, but credible.)

When we met again, I consciously decided to foster a different approach: given our recent success, our companies should work together as partners. But I never got a chance to say it – the chairman brought it up first.

(*Third impression:* McCormack knows when to say yes.)

Every once in a while you find yourself at a first meeting where you are creating dozens of positive impressions. Everything you say works. The chemistry is perfect. Every idea clicks.

These are the most dangerous first impressions – because they create high expectations for future encounters.

I once had lunch with a European executive who had just been appointed head of US operations of one of our oldest and biggest customers. It was a get-acquainted lunch, nothing more. At the least, I hoped to find out his interests; at best, I hoped to expose him to one or two projects in our pipeline.

The conversation that ensued was amazing. In the course of ninety minutes we discussed matters that normally would take several meetings to discover.

By the main course, we had established that we had mutual friends in his native country, that we saw eye to eye on his country's political problems, that he loved golf, that he would be in Great Britain in July and he could be my guest at the British Open, and that I was good friends with his company's largest shareholder.

If I had scripted the dialogue to portray myself in a favourable light, I could not have done any better.

As dessert and coffee were served, we began talking about the company brand with which we most likely would be associated. He mentioned he had just visited the brand's headquarters in Europe.

I remarked that our company owned a golf school in that town. To my astonishment, he replied, 'Yes, I know. My son is going there next month.'

'What's his name?' I asked. 'I'll make sure he's treated well.'

I left that lunch confident that I had made a very favourable first impression. But I'll bet all the goodwill would have come to nothing had I not made a good second impression: I remembered to check up on his son a few weeks later at our golf school.

A great first impression is meaningless if you don't follow it with an equally great second one, and a third one, and a fourth one . . .

When to Show Off Your Memory

Most people don't give themselves sufficient credit for having a good memory. And even fewer people have the confidence or skill to display their memory to their advantage.

Nearly everybody, in one form or another, has a good memory. Some people remember cooking recipes. Others remember baseball statistics. Some people have photographic memories. Others have extremely selective ones; they can remember phone numbers or jokes or birthdays but not what they had for breakfast.

People who know me well will tell you that I have an impressive memory. Over the years I've startled some of our athlete clients by being able to recall a birdie they shot on the fifteenth hole in the third round of the Greater Hartford Open in 1979 or the backhand winner that pulled them out of a second-set tie-breaker in the semifinals of a tennis tournament in Oklahoma City.

Notice that I said I have an *impressive* memory, not a remarkable one. There is a difference. A remarkable memory means you can remember a lot of things. An impressive memory means you can dazzle people with the few things you do remember.

The truth is that I have a very selective memory. I remember small things rather than big things. If I'm good at the minutiae of sports, I'm not so good at recalling our golf division's gross revenues, even though I may have seen the numbers last week. You'd think that in the normal scheme of things, the revenues of one of our biggest divisions would be easier to remember than a birdie in Hartford two decades back. But that's not how my mind works.

Still, I have learned to get the most from my memory. Under the right circumstances, I'm not ashamed to show it off. If I do it well, people will attribute to me greater mental powers than I probably deserve – and that's an advantage in business or in life.

For example, I have always made a point of knowing our second- and third-tier clients. It is important for me to keep in touch with up-and-coming clients because someday they may become top clients and they will attract others.

That is where my selective memory comes in handy. If I can say to a sixteen-year-old tennis player who is ranked 120th in the world, 'Gee, that was a tough second set in your quarterfinal doubles match at Wichita' or 'I see that your shoe contract is up for renewal and I have some ideas about what we should do', that little display comes back in multiples to benefit our company.

Not only does it present me as someone who cares about tennis in general and that player in particular, but the same impression might filter down to other players and tennis officials. Ultimately, it may sway a young player or a national federation to sign with us rather than a competitor.

The line between impressing people with your memory and showing off is a fine one, however. So be careful. In my youth I memorized the names of all the train stations between Chicago and Champaign, Illinois. I still know them. But I haven't employed this parlour trick since junior high school.

The best time to display your memory is when other people are in a position to challenge it.

A few years ago an associate and I had a meeting at Coca-Cola's Atlanta headquarters. One of the Coca-Cola executives showed up with a laptop computer to type in the notes of our meeting. The laptop was a first for me and I was a little amused

113

by it. But then I started to think about what it implied. It occurred to me that anyone who takes notes on such a fancy piece of hardware would probably be very precise about what was said in a meeting. I made a mental note to be equally precise.

The next time we met, the executive again showed up with his laptop computer. I began the meeting by summarizing with as much detail as possible the substance of our previous discussion. As I delivered my five-minute oration, I could see Mr Laptop scrolling through his computer, comparing his notes with mine. When I finished, he looked up from his screen, nodded in my direction, and said, 'Mark, you didn't miss a thing.' By itself, showing that I had a good memory was certainly not enough to make or break the sale. But I have to believe that it improved the credibility of what I said thereafter.

Everybody, whether a CEO or a student, likes to display their powers of recall.

When we remember a colleague's birthday, we make sure the colleague knows it. When we recall a pertinent bit of information during a meeting, we expect a little credit for it. When we remember a fact that everyone else has forgotten, we're not shy about congratulating ourselves.

Nor do you need a particularly agile or retentive mind to harness the power of your memory. Qute often, the deft use of a document can suggest you have a better memory than you really do.

For example, my wife Betsy is a photo fanatic. She never travels without a pocket camera and takes thousands of pictures a year. She gets two sets developed, keeps one set for her scrapbooks and sends the duplicate to whoever is in the picture. In and of itself, it's no big deal. It is not particularly unique; lots of people do the same thing with snapshots from weddings, vacations or family celebrations. It is a kind, thoughtful gesture; there is no hidden motive.

Yet I'm sure that the people receiving those photos credit Betsy with a far better memory than she may possess. By remembering to send a photo of the event, she gets credit for remembering the event itself without actually having to recall the details

114

and spell them out in a long letter. I know this is true because of the increased regard I have for friends who send *me* pictures.

If the simple, uncalculated act of sending photos has such a favourable impact, imagine the effect of a carefully predetermined use of documents.

Most of us, before an important meeting with a client or customer, have enough sense to dig into our files to refresh our memory about that particular relationship. After all, we never know what we'll find, and we might even learn something.

But how many of us have the sense actually to pull out the documents and use them to jog the other side's memory? This can be very effective.

I once had a session with an executive who was one of our company's first customers. I had not seen him in several years and thought it was time we talked face-to-face again. During the meeting, he stunned me by his near-total recall of our early dealings together.

'In fact,' he said, 'I have a two-inch thick file of correspondence on the first sale you ever made to our company. I thought you'd be interested in seeing it.'

With that, he handed me a complete copy of the file – notes, letters, contract drafts, matchbooks from restaurants where we had lunched twenty years before. I was genuinely moved by the gesture, not so much because the documents were fascinating (which they were) but because he had kept them and remembered.

Even a modest display of memory can strengthen a relationship. It shows that you care.

You Don't Get Credit for Being Prepared – but You Do Get Results

I've never met a successful person who wasn't 100% prepared. Once you realize the edge exceptional preparation gives, it becomes a lifelong habit.

Ivan Lendl is a case in point. He has thought about every aspect of his game, whether it is a playing strategy against an opponent, or his diet, or fitness regime or when he schedules his naps. That attitude touches every aspect of his life.

The first time I met Ivan, I was impressed that he knew precisely where he was going to be in six months' time, even though this is not uncommon for a top performer. But he floored me by also knowing the airline and flight number he was taking to the city in question. That is the way he goes about everything. It is one ingredient that has made him a champion.

Jackie Stewart, too, is always meticulously prepared. If he says he will meet you eleven weeks from Monday at 10.30 at your Chicago office, you have no need to reconfirm the appointment. Jackie will be there. Much of this, I am sure, he picked up during his racing career, where checking the safety and performance details before he took the wheel was a matter of life or death. Jackie has never abandoned that discipline in his other pursuits. He has high standards and doesn't move until all his questions are answered.

One reason many of us aren't prepared is that we rarely get credit for it. Preparation is something we do outside the spotlight. And if anyone *does* find out we have prepared intensively to make certain we achieve our goal, we may well be teased and told we're too uptight – it is not 'cool' to be a grind.

In fact, many people are afraid to be prepared: if they are, they lose an excellent excuse when they fail.

In sports, you encounter athletes who let it be known they are not in top condition for a tournament or game. It relieves the pressure. If they lose, they were not at their best. If they win, they exceed everyone's expectations. This is a classic 50% solution: You win some, you lose some.

Then there are the people who do their preparation in public. They constantly tell you how hard they are working. That way, if they fail, it is not because they didn't try. This is the 75% solution: Prepare well, give it your best, let the chips fall where they may.

116

Consummate performers, however, spend hidden hours to assure that they are No. 1. They don't need or want the world to see them sweat.

Ballet dancers train eight hours a day for years so their spins and leaps on stage look effortless.

Sir Laurence Olivier would spend weeks memorizing his lines until he could recite them without thinking. Only then would he start to rehearse a play.

When Christie Brinkley was the top model in the world, shooting the cover of *Sports Illustrated*'s swimsuit issue, she would schedule her wake-up call at 2 a.m. knowing that unless she put icepacks on her eyes, which always swelled with sleep, she would not look good enough when the sun broke over the horizon. That was when the light was soft, the tones flattering and the photographer was ready to shoot. This is the 110% solution: First determine the desired result. *Then* calculate your effort.

People have all sorts of rituals that constitute legitimate preparation. Sometimes excellent preparation can be as mundane as taking notes. I once knew a man who was an able technician but not a naturally talented sports photographer. He simply worked every angle so that he would become the best, and he succeeded. He kept a notebook showing precisely when and where the field went into shadow in every major stadium in America during the football season. From that, he knew where to position himself as a game progressed and what side of the field would give him the most dramatic results.

Some preparation rituals can be slightly exotic. Bobby Locke, the great South African golfer who won the British Open four times, used to wake up on the day of a tournament and do everything – getting dressed, eating breakfast, brushing his teeth – in painfully slow motion. Lacing his golf shoes sometimes took ten minutes. Every movement was calculated to get him into a slow tempo for the golf course.

A lot of athletes nowadays are keen on the technique known as visualization. A champion figure skater such as Brian Orser will mentally run through every part of his programme before going on the ice. If he can complete a difficult move in his mind, he is more likely to repeat it while performing.

This notion isn't new. Years ago, an injury prevented Jean-Claude Killy from skiing before a giant slalom race. So he studied films of the course and mentally rehearsed going through every gate at the fastest speed. He won.

Golfers like Jack Nicklaus will tell you that before they ever hit a golf ball, they see it arcing through the air and landing on the grass; then they swing.

First the result. Then the effort.

That is more or less the way I prepare for an important meeting. I visualize everyone in the room smiling, in agreement, shaking hands. And then I work my way backwards to decide how I got there.

Not too long ago a sporting federation that had been a long-time client of ours began to treat us badly during renewal talks. Its behaviour, by my lights, was professionally unwise. And on a personal level, I thought it was rude.

I was mad, and I knew I had to voice my displeasure to the group's leader one-on-one.

Now in my younger days, my impulse would have been to leap to the phone and vent my anger at whoever had done me wrong. The other party might be infuriated or intimidated, but he would certainly know how I felt.

The problem with that strategy was that I didn't have a clue if they would be infuriated or intimidated. I had gauged the effort, but not the result. That's not good preparation.

In this case, I decided that since I was personally affronted, I should keep the meeting on a personal level. So I invited the federation head to my home in Cleveland.

That decision dictated everything that followed. For one thing, no matter what I said, I knew our meeting would at least end on a polite and friendly note. He was, after all, a guest in my home. So I prepared for that result.

I showed him around the house. I served him lunch. Then we retired to my study where I launched into some very aggressive remarks, at the same time apologizing for doing so.

'I'm going to tell you exactly what's on my mind, and I'm sorry if it upsets you. I am irritated at the way this matter has been handled . . .'

I had rehearsed my litany of complaints and knew the order in which I would present them. As I sailed from one injustice to another, he visibly blanched.

I was prepared for a confrontation.

After walking through my house, eating my food and settling comfortably in my study, he was not.

I had planned to end the meeting on a conciliatory note, so I beat a hasty retreat. I outlined some upbeat constructive steps he could take that would mollify me and work to his advantage. Having played out the scenario the way I intended, we parted as friends. And he remains a client.

Do I Barge Through or Beg?

Several years ago I gave a ride to a carful of tennis people going from Como in Italy to Lugano in Switzerland. There was a long line of cars at the Italian–Swiss border. The border guards apparently were checking everyone's travel documents. Seeing this, one of my passengers alerted me that her passport had recently expired.

For a moment I panicked, envisioning all of us being detained for hours at the border. I turned to everyone in the car and said, 'I don't know how to deal with this situation. Should I barge through or beg?'

I was still mulling this over as I pulled the car up to the checkpoint.

Then, in my most polite and deferential tone, I told the guard who we were, where we were going and the passport problem we had just discovered – and without even looking at our papers, he waved us through.

In other words, I begged.

Time and time again, I've learned that this is the best and

119

only way to deal with the dozens of gatekeepers, clerks and authoritarians you encounter every day.

My wife Betsy seems to know this instinctively. She has a knack for making people want to do things for her – because she knows the value of recognizing people's authority and letting them display it.

Consider this small but telling example.

You are standing in a long line for tickets at a movie theatre. The movie is about to begin, and there is an even longer line of people inside the theatre waiting to buy popcorn and drinks. If you want those too, there is a good chance that you will miss the start.

Do you barge through or beg?

Some people always try to barge through. They will be frank with the ticket-taker, but not deferential.

'My husband is queuing,' they say, 'and I want to go in for some popcorn. He'll be with you in a minute' – as if that is sufficient reason to breeze by. The ticket-taker, of course, stops them cold – because they have flouted his authority. They have trifled with the one thing he controls, namely, who gets through and who doesn't. And so he exercises his authority. They don't get in.

My wife is a master at maximizing people's authority. She will say, 'I know this isn't right, but my husband is in the queue over there. There's a long queue for popcorn and I don't want to miss the movie. Could you possibly let me through?' Invariably, the ticket-taker says, 'Go ahead'. (Translation: 'I've used my authority to let you cross the line.')

People in authority, high or low, like you to recognize their clout. If you do and give them a chance to demonstrate it, they almost always will do so in your favour.

I suspect we pick up this instinct as children – from the major authority figures in our life, our parents. As children, we sense that our parents expect us to be in a perpetual state of deference to their authority.

It is not a matter of life or death for our parents if we want to have an extra cookie, or invite a friend to the house, or turn on the television. They usually grant permission without thinking. The point is, as they are forever reminding us, it would be nice to be asked.

But we change as we get older, perhaps because the authority figures in our lives are less clearly defined. Suddenly they are not our obvious elders and betters (our parents, teachers and coaches) but people whom we may regard as our equals or our inferiors. And so, because of arrogance or insensitivity, we resist them.

This dynamic is most obvious in the workplace – between subordinate and boss. If you resist the boss, you are doomed. This is true whether you are talented, productive or right when the boss is wrong.

And yet if you yield ever so slightly to the boss's authority, it can work wonders. As a boss myself, I know that I will give our people tremendous latitude to take chances and blunder, as long as they ask me about it beforehand.

This dynamic, which we so readily accepted as children, remains unchanged in a host of everyday situations.

That ticket-taker at the movie theatre may be nineteen years old and earning one-twentieth your salary, but for those brief moments when you want to get through to the popcorn line, he is the most important person in your world. And you should treat him that way. Likewise with the border guard I encountered at the Italian–Swiss frontier.

If you place yourself on the mercy of the court, the court is more likely to show mercy.

Writing Proposals That Get Read

I still write many of our company's sales proposals. I should probably delegate more of this but, frankly, a proposal over my signature has a greater chance of being read at a company that doesn't know us well. Here is a quick course on writing proposals:

Keep them short

Before you mail your twenty-four-page masterpiece, ask yourself: When was the last time you got as far as page twenty-four of someone else's proposal?

Give them your best ideas, not all your ideas

A proposal is often judged by the worst idea in it; at least, that's the one someone at the target company always seems to pick on. You never get a second chance to send a first proposal. Save your off-the-wall suggestions for later when they know you better.

Remember your reader

A person's rank says a lot about how you should communicate with them. As a general rule, CEOs and senior executives want strategic solutions (Why should we do this? What long-term problem does it solve?). Vice-presidents want tactical answers (What will this cost? How will it simplify my life?). Junior people want technical details (How does it work? Will it fit? Will it last?). Tailor your proposal with that in mind.

Canvass your colleagues

When it comes to proposals, it's foolish to work alone. I'm always asking our executives for a dozen ideas, each appropriate for a new prospect. I then cherry-pick the best suggestions and drop them into my proposal.

Create an inside track

My favourite proposals are the ones I don't have to write. Instead, an associate addresses a memo to me on what XYZ Corp should be doing, and I send it on to the company with a covering letter saying, in effect, 'Here are some of our internal thoughts, which you might find interesting.' It gives our proposal the aura of inside information – and it always gets read.

When Paper Is a Problem

The daily confrontation with too many memos, letters, forms and reports is a common complaint in business. And paper trails have only become longer because of those modern marvels, the word processor, the fax and overnight deliveries.

I won't argue with the standard advice for coping with paper-work: *only touch a piece of paper once*. Act on it, delegate it, file it or throw it away. But this advice assumes an ideal world, one in which everybody responds exactly as you want them to.

Here are a few practical strategies for dealing with paperwork in an imperfect world.

Know thyself

There are two types of people – the ones who dread paperwork and the ones who thrive on it.

If you are the former, the first step is to admit this to yourself. The second step: find a subordinate who fits into the latter category and let him or her handle the paper. This is a doubly efficient solution: you've not only delegated a distasteful part of your job, but you've assigned it to the most qualified person.

People who love paperwork have a more serious problem than those who hate it – namely, tearing themselves away from their desk and files and getting some real work done. If I recognized this trait in myself, I would discipline myself to limit sharply the time I spent on paperwork.

Never send a memo to just one person

Put your message in writing only if it's intended for two or more people. If you need to communicate with one person, and no one else, pick up the phone.

Obviously, there are times when a memo to one person is the most appropriate form of communication – when you can't reach the individual by phone, for example, or when you need to communicate complicated information. But I suspect that a more aggressive use of the phone – as opposed to the use of memos as a form of aggression – could eliminate half the paperwork in most organizations.

Scribble in the margins

The best way to respond to a document, internal or external, that asks you to do something is to scribble a one-liner on the document itself and shuffle it back to its author.

A mundane example: publications often write to us for permission to reprint material from my monthly newsletter, *Success Secrets*. We could draft a formal letter asserting our copyright interests and granting or denying permission each time we received such a request. Instead, we scribble 'permission granted' on the request, keep a copy and send it back. It's perfectly legal, it gets the job done and it saves everyone a lot of time.

This technique applies even to internal paperwork, where formality and cosmetics are rarely an issue. Not enough younger executives have picked up the habit, perhaps because they don't have the confidence or authority to scribble in the margins or they feel that doing so will appear arrogant. Instead, they needlessly process more paper – by drafting a response, attaching it to the original, making a copy for their files and sending it off – as if someone were grading them on how neatly they adhered to some imagined rules of corporate communication.

Believe me, the rules are very lax and no one is grading your neatness or penmanship. If I got one of my memos back from a junior executive with a pithy note in the margin, I wouldn't be offended. I'd be relieved.

Consider taping messages

Perhaps the best way to trim the paperwork in your life is to resist paper altogether. John Dolan, an attorney and accomplished public speaker who presented my book, *What They Don't Teach You at Harvard Business School*, as a seminar, relies on audio-cassettes rather than paper.

Because he is constantly on the road, Dolan lacks the most essential piece of equipment for generating paperwork: an office. His solution, however, is ingenious and perfectly suited to his talents as a speaker. Wherever he may be, Dolan dictates his reports and memos on individual cassettes and mails them to his secretary in California. The secretary doesn't waste time transcribing the tapes on to paper. Instead, she sends a copy of the cassette to the appropriate party.

These audio memos not only save time, they eliminate the risk that something will be lost in transcription. Most important, unlike written memos where the message is open to several interpretations, the tapes are not ambiguous. Listeners hearing Dolan's inflections and emphasis on certain subjects pick up all the nuances in his message. They know exactly what he is trying to say. Of course, Dolan is in the kind of business where he needs to keep no record of what he has said or done. That is quite a luxury.

Spring-clean your files

At least once a year, have your assistant weed the files – and you should take a few hours to look over his or her shoulder. You will be appalled at the number of useless records and files that have accumulated. Then try and resolve to keep less paper in the future. This will save an astonishing amount of effort – and money. It will also endear you to your secretary, who hates filing.

First Influence, Then Authority

At some point in your career you may well find yourself in that no man's land between being a boss and being among the bossed. You have influence, but you do not have the authority that goes with it. Others listen to you, but they are not required to do your bidding.

Some people find this grey area confusing and frustrating. I once saw it derail the career and fortune of a partner at a small New York investment group.

The firm was dominated by a senior partner who held sway over a dozen other bright and energetic partners. It did not take long for the senior partner to see that my friend was just a little bit smarter than his associates, even though they were ostensibly equal in rank. His ideas were bolder, his contacts better and his deals considerably more profitable.

The senior partner began grooming the young man. He introduced him to his powerful friends. He helped him become a trustee of a prestigious museum. He habitually deferred to him at partnership meetings. In deed, if not by actual word, he confirmed that the young partner had become first among his equals.

However, the absence of a verbal confirmation began to gnaw at the young man. He wasn't satisfied with the commanding lead he had gained over his rivals. He wanted the stripes to prove it.

He eventually confronted the senior partner over this, saying in effect, 'Tell them I'm in charge.' The older man, realizing the chaos such an announcement would cause, naturally refused.

As for the young partner, the frustration of having influence without authority was more than he could bear. He eventually left the firm.

Here are some suggestions on how to exercise your influence so that you eventually acquire the commensurate authority.

1. Believe the signals

I can understand why many people are poor at gauging their influence. It is not something that is easily measured, nor is it

126

something that most bosses disclose explicitly. Bosses do not ordinarily come up to you in the hallway, slap you on the back and say, 'Hey, I trust you.'

Some people are oblivious to the fact that they have influence. You see this quite often in younger employees who do not always appreciate that, despite their lack of seniority, they are being listened to.

The head of a small advertising agency once told me about a talented woman, fresh out of college, who worked in his art department and almost destroyed the operation.

It was clear very quickly that, as an art director, she was a budding superstar. Her designs were beautiful, she had exquisite taste, she knew exactly what she wanted – and she wasn't afraid to express her opinion.

That was the problem. In creative departments people are always judging one another's work to see whether, say, a piece of advertising is good enough to show to a client. Over time, if they care about keeping their friends, they learn how to criticize a creation without destroying its creator.

Not this woman. She was blunt, almost as if she didn't think anyone was listening. But because she was talented, people did listen.

For the sake of in-house harmony, her boss finally had to take her aside and explain that she simply had to be more tactful, that she could not shoot off her mouth as if what she said carried no weight.

'Until that moment,' the agency head told me, 'I am positive she didn't have a clue as to how influential she really was.'

Take an honest look at yourself in group situations. How do people respond to you? Has their attitude changed over time?

In your community, have you noticed that your neighbours include you more frequently in their activities? Are they phoning you more often at home to get your advice? Have you been asked to volunteer your professional expertise in some way on behalf of the community? These are small signals, but they indicate that your influence is growing.

At work, do people defer to you in meetings – or cut you off abruptly? Do colleagues regularly come to you for help – or do you go to them? Are the documents that cross your desk asking for an opinion – or are they telling you to carry out someone else's decision? Are you invited to meetings on subjects outside your specific area?

Learn to recognize the signals that indicate your importance, not only your rank.

2. Be a calming influence

I attended a public meeting not long ago on a controversial issue. The meeting teetered on the edge of chaos. Everyone, it seemed, had an opinion and demanded to be heard. It wasn't long before the sides were clearly drawn, the volume escalated, people began shouting at one another and rational debate was abandoned.

Then something extraordinary happened. While the combatants were catching their breath, an unprepossessing woman stood up and in a soft, evenly modulated voice offered her view on the subject. The room quieted as everyone attempted to hear her barely audible voice. Although she was articulate, it was the manner rather than the substance of her statement that made such a strong impression. Amid all the shouting, she turned out to be an island of calm and reason. And that influenced the rest of the meeting.

Being the calm voice is a wise strategy in almost any situation. The more heated the other party is, the cooler you should be. If you can keep your head while all those around you are losing theirs, your authority will always exceed theirs.

3. Stick to the point

Some people get emotionally carried away in group situations. Others lose their intellectual bearings. They cannot stick to the point. They get sidetracked on secondary issues. As a result, they lose attention and respect. Worse, they lose control.

One of the easiest ways to influence a situation is to help the participants stay on the subject. People gravitate not only to the wise person but to the disciplined one as well.

4. Be a self-starter

Don't rely on someone else's initiative. Take the initiative yourself. In most group situations the person who initiates a project or concept usually becomes the authority in that area.

I have seen this happen repeatedly in our company. A few years back one of the senior management people in our London office suggested that we should be producing opera extravaganzas around the world.

I don't pretend to know much about opera, other than that Sir Thomas Beecham said 'God has yet to invent a faster way of spending money than putting on an opera.' It seemed like a risky idea to me, but since we had located a partner, the impresario Harvey Goldsmith, we let them take a shot at it with a production of Verdi's *Aida* at Earls Court in London. The production was a success and subsequently the instigators of the idea produced *Carmen* in London and then took it to both Japan and Australia.

5. Praise people

Praise is a subtle and wonderfully effective way to gain influence over people.

It is effective because three things happen when you praise someone: (1) the person likes hearing it; (2) he likes you for saying it; and (3) he wants to hear more.

It is subtle because few people notice how they have become addicted to your praise or how you have established yourself as an arbiter of good and bad in their lives. Your praise, of course, must be genuine and deserved. Anything less will seem insidious and manipulative. If you can remember to praise people when the situation warrants it, you will not only lift their spirits, you will lift your own chances of having a successful career.

129

6. Pick your spots

The most consistent winners have a keen sense of the balance between their influence and their authority. They do not assert themselves without picking their spots carefully. When they overstep their authority, they usually have a good idea that their influence can justify it.

One of our junior executives arrived at Kennedy Airport and noticed the marketing chief of a major corporation in the first-class line for the flight to London. Our executive immediately upgraded his ticket to first class – a privilege not accorded our executives – so that he could sit next to the marketing chief. When he submitted his expenses, he instructed the accounting department to reimburse him for the upgrade because a big sale might well result from the flight. He did not have the authority to do that, but a few months later when a deal came through it was clear that he had not misjudged his influence.

7. Don't rush the process

Gaining influence, like establishing your credibility or winning someone's trust, is something that happens slowly, so slowly that many of us don't notice it. But the clues are there.

Consider the relationship between a golf pro and his caddy. The first time the pro asks the caddy, 'What do you think I ought to hit?' the caddy might answer, 'It's 165 yards to the front of the green.' In effect, the caddy is saying, 'You decide.'

But as they work together, the caddy gets bolder about club selection. If the caddy is good and if the pro regularly accepts his suggestions, he will eventually just pull a five-iron from the bag and hand it to the pro. What has happened is never stated explicitly, but the caddy has assumed a position of influence and acts on it.

You see the same dynamic in dozens of everyday situations. Mechanics are solicitous the first time you bring in your car. They point out what is probably wrong, what parts they may need to replace and why. But after a few visits, when it is clear

130

that you are a satisfied customer, they simply assume that they have your approval to do whatever is necessary.

Interior designers are very alert to this dynamic (at least the ones we hire for our offices). At first, they are deferential. They call you up, show you pictures and discuss every detail in an effort to get a fix on your taste. But once they sense they have your confidence, they take the initiative. Instead of saying, 'Here is a photo of a table that might be nice for your conference room, what do you think?' they declare, 'Here is the table we are buying for your conference room.'

I think this is good, especially if the authority they take means that they are working at their creative best and are not bothering me with details.

You have to be careful, however. When my wife and I were building our home in Florida, I casually mentioned to the architects that we were thinking about including a poolhouse and wondered what would be involved. I thought they would sketch something out on a scrap of paper. But they returned with a full-blown presentation and a $25,000 bill for the design work. I never asked for that. They overstepped their authority and lost some of their influence – and a good bit of money – in the process.

8. Act as if you have influence

As a general rule, if you want to become the boss, start acting like one.

The people who get ahead are not necessarily smarter. They simply have a better understanding of their influence and they are not afraid to exercise it. While their rivals are making a recommendation, the winners are already in action.

One of the more dramatic examples of this in our company occurred in the mid-1980s. James Erskine, the head of our Australian operations, committed our company to buying an office building in Sydney before he obtained the proper authorization.

Now, I don't care how big you are, buying a building is a major decision in any organization. There are finance committees, corporate officers and bank officials who have to sign off on the transaction.

But Erskine was half-way around the world and had only a few hours to close the deal. He called me up and explained what he had to do and why. His position was, 'This is such a good buy that if it doesn't work out, I'll find a way to buy it myself.'

How could I argue with that? I said, 'Fine'. Of course, the technocrats in our company were appalled. But it turned out to be a brilliant decision. As for James Erskine, he didn't lose any career points by his unorthodox methods. On the contrary, he gained even more authority. He now runs all of our operations in Australia and Southeast Asia – from the building he bought in Sydney.

CHAPTER SEVEN

Ideas that Win

Good ideas come in many sizes, and a great small idea is often as brilliant as a great big idea. People have a tendency to concentrate so much on the large picture that they miss out on significant opportunities.

Let me give an example. Many of us wish we had invented plastic. That spawned dozens of industries and generated billions and billions of dollars. That was a big idea. But other smaller ideas followed. For example, plastic wrapping for food.

Someone else shaped the plastic into sacks, so that instead of merely wrapping leftovers you could enclose them. A good and profitable notion. Another inventor bonded paper on to bits of wire, creating the baggy-tie, which has become a staple item everywhere. After that came airtight freezer bags that seal across the top. And consider the multitude of garbage bags now on our supermarket shelves. There seems to be no end to the uses of plastic.

A great big idea has any number of great small ideas within it, waiting to be discovered. It is usually a mistake to imagine that the string of smaller ideas has been used up; often, that string can be extended almost indefinitely.

Fresh Eyes

In the majority of cases, new ideas address old problems. A problem is really an opportunity for a solution. Why and how a person comes up with a solution usually has to do with fresh eyes.

Always try to look at a problem as if for the first time. Forget the ways it has been handled in the past. Take nothing for granted – except the assumption that a solution can be found.

For example, a few years back an immigrant, new to southern California, noticed that almost everyone there wore sunglasses. At the same time, he heard complaints about the heat in parked cars and how the upholstery could be burning hot from the glare of the sun. So this man started marketing sunglasses for cars. He designed reflective panels that sat on top of the dashboard and kept the heat out. Using a catchy visual metaphor, he had sunglasses printed on the reflective material. The idea, one hopes, made the inventor wealthy.

So use fresh eyes to find a need – and fill it.

Open and Closed Ideas

Remember the Pet Rock? That was a popular item many years ago. It was just a small rock in a box and, if I remember correctly, the rock came with a booklet explaining the reason for having a rock as a pet.

The Pet Rock probably cost a few cents to package and market but it sold for several dollars. On a percentage rate of return, it was probably as profitable as the explosive early days of Xerox. The Pet Rock, however, was a closed idea. It didn't lead to anything else. When it was over, it was over.

Open ideas are superior to closed ones.

It's like evolution. The platypus may be a perfectly delightful creature, but it is an evolutionary dead end. It is the Pet Rock of the animal kingdom.

The first dog, on the other hand, gave rise to perhaps a

thousand breeds – one for every purpose and personal taste. That's what an open idea is like. Open ideas lead to multiple applications and transformations. If you can make a big score with a quick one-shot idea, that's terrific. But if you want a durable, expanding base, then think in terms of ideas that keep on going.

The Tangible and the Intangible

Ideas are abstract; it is much easier to talk about them in terms of how they are expressed in material form. But don't get the impression that ideas in material form are the only ones that matter. If that were true, then only a tiny percentage of us would be able to benefit from our ideas. Very few of us, after all, will ever hold a patent or have a brainchild that will end up being manufactured.

Intangible ideas are every bit as valuable as ones that manifest themselves in physical form. Intangible ideas are close to my heart because they are what IMG is about. Service, our core business, is built on abstract notions: understanding what people really want and sensing where the opportunities will be.

These are the crucial components of an intangible idea that works.

Understanding What People Really Want

There are two ways to convince people that your idea is of value. You can tell them about it. Or you can show them. Telling, no matter how well or subtly you do it, comes down to making a sales pitch; and sales pitches put people on guard.

Showing people what your idea can do for them makes them more receptive. They feel they are getting a no-obligation opportunity to sense your style and your level of competence.

In order to show people what you can do for them, however,

135

you've got to have a canny sense of what they want. What people really want is not always what they seem to want, and what you can really do for them is not necessarily at the heart of your idea as *you* see it.

Let me tell you about the beginning of my relationship with Arnold Palmer. He was sceptical about having a manager and he had a right to be. The idea had never been tested; it had never been proven that a business manager could do a professional golfer one iota of good.

Arnold and I held a number of preliminary conversations while I was still a practising attorney in Cleveland, Ohio. I told him about the opportunities I saw on the horizon – the endorsements, licensing deals and exhibitions. Arnold listened politely but held himself aloof.

What I failed to realize was that Arnold was not primarily money-motivated. Through the years, he has become an extraordinarily savvy businessman, making hundreds of millions of dollars. He now owns country clubs and several aviation companies; his automobile dealerships are among the largest in the United States with 1989 sales of $900 million. He also has the largest golf course design and construction company in the world, with more than forty courses currently in the works.

But it has always been the accomplishment and not the money that motivates Arnold, and back in 1960 his sense of accomplishment was focused with great discipline and single-mindedness on playing golf as well as the game could possibly be played. If he did that, he believed the other things would fall into place.

In other words what he really wanted was not someone to help him make a lot of money, but someone to help him simplify and organize his life so that he could concentrate on his sport.

Once I figured that out, it was relatively easy to find a way to show him what I could do for him. I got my chance one night at the Palmer home in Latrobe, Pennsylvania, where Arnold, his wife Winnie and I had just had dinner. Arnold and I went into his study and he motioned in despair towards his desk. 'That's what drives me crazy,' he said. There was a mountain of un-

136

opened mail. 'That's what I come home to after every tournament.'

Well, Arnold and I talked on, but the subject didn't matter.
I was just biding my time until he got tired and announced that
he was going to bed. After he turned in, I attacked his desk.

I spent half the night going through hundreds of pieces of
mail, everything from fan letters and charity solicitations to
supermarket circulars and business propositions.

The next morning Arnold woke up to a neat, nearly bare desk,
with only three short stacks of correspondence for his attention.
'Arnold,' I said, 'forget the money. This is what professional
management can do for you.' And that is what he wanted:
simplicity, organization, peace of mind.

Sensing Where the Opportunities Will Be

A crucial concept in any sort of business planning is the pipeline.
For a moment, take this figure of speech literally and talk about
the idea pipeline as if it were an oil pipeline. In both cases
nothing happens until the basic commodity – crude oil or smart
idea – is located and dug up. But this basic commodity is not
ready to be shown to the world: it has to be refined, purified and
adapted to optimum efficiency for its end use. This takes time.
Finally, it has to be delivered to the customer. This takes more
time. And whether we're talking about petroleum or about ideas,
what makes or breaks you are not the market conditions on the
day you dig up your commodity, but the conditions on the date
the product is presented for sale. Having a bright idea today
isn't good enough. It's got to be a bright idea the day after
tomorrow.

In this, there is no small component of dumb luck. None of
us – and no idea – escapes the force of circumstance. If we
succeed, part of our success should be attributed to chance.

Luck can be our ally or our nemesis, and what is usually called
intuition can be equally well defined as a knack for getting luck
on your side.

137

I'll pass along a quote from the poet Virgil: 'Fortune favours the bold.' An idea that is meek today will seem downright wimpy tomorrow. But an idea that seems overly bold today will probably seem just about right next year.

If an idea is truly new, it's bound to be resisted. If it isn't resisted, chances are it isn't truly new.

Is There Anything New Under the Sun?

Ideas build on other ideas. They take older notions as their foundation and add new stories to the edifice. In this respect, even the most ruggedly individualistic among us is in some sense dependent on and beholden to others.

I stress this because individualism is a Western tradition and we sometimes lose sight of the interdependence of ideas. We tend to think of ourselves as working alone, creating alone, inventing alone. While this tradition is a noble and courageous one, it has its dangers. We sometimes give short shrift to the concepts of teamwork and cooperation. As recent history has shown, this can hurt our competitive position *vis-à-vis* other cultures where greater emphasis is placed on working together.

In the name of 110% effectiveness, we've got to recognize that ideas are there to be used by all of us. This certainly does not mean that it is all right to appropriate the ideas of others. What it does mean is that we should be less hung up on originality for its own sake and more sensitive to improving ideas that already exist.

If you invent a product, and I come up with an innovative way to package it, haven't I also made a contribution? If I come up with a process or application that makes your brainchild 5% or 10% more valuable, haven't I accomplished something that reflects well on both of us?

You can never translate the customs of one culture into another culture, and I'm not suggesting we try. However, we should recognize the different ways in which ideas can be exploited. All of us have heard the cliché that the Japanese don't originate ideas, they only refine them. For the Japanese, refining the idea *is* the idea. Refinement is necessarily the work of many minds and many pairs of hands. And refinement of the idea enjoys equal prestige with conceiving the idea.

In the West, the emphasis is quite different. We reserve our greatest glory for the originator; those who build on the idea and perfect it – who make it work – are rarely given appropriate credit.

The Realistic Idea and the Moonshot

The realistic notion shows that you have a street-smart understanding of what makes your business tick. It makes it clear that you realize an idea must be implemented before it does anyone any good.

The moonshot – having a Head of State attend your town meeting – shows a certain boldness of mind and the excellence of what you might produce. Might, however, is the operative word. Moonshots, therefore, should never be promised. They should always be presented hypothetically: 'It would be great if we could . . . A pet dream of mine is . . . Something I'd love to take a shot at is. . .'.

Phrases like those convey passion without making promises. They create a framework in which realistic notions can be executed and in which moonshots can be dreamed of and worked towards.

The best ideas are bold and *realizable. A mix of attainable goals and moonshots is the surest sign of an active and fruitful imagination.*

Does the Idea Fit?

Sometimes people work so hard that they lose all sense of what it is they are working towards. Besides, defining a group or

139

company's central idea is more difficult than you might think.

Take IMG. You might say that the central idea of IMG is sports. After all, our company started out in sports and that is the field with which we're still most closely identified.

If sports is the core of our business, then maybe we ought to have a division manufacturing sporting goods. We know the market. We've got top professionals who can advise us on product design. And we've got an impressive stable of in-house endorsers. So, at first glance, getting into the sporting goods business seems like a pretty good idea.

In fact, it might be disastrous. We have never dealt in products. We don't know how to execute a manufacturing idea. And established sporting goods companies provide a significant amount of the business we do on behalf of our clients. We would have to think very carefully about it before being seen to be going into competition with them.

That suggests that sports is not really at the core of our company.

So let's try again. IMG began by representing athletes, and increasingly during the past quarter-century athletes have become celebrities. So maybe IMG is in the celebrity business.

If this is so, we might as well get involved with all kinds of celebrities. Why not rock stars? We know how to stage events. We know how to arrange venues and sell tickets. And rock stars make a lot of money.

But again, this might be a terrible idea for us. We don't know how the rock world works – and, frankly, we perhaps don't want to know. We offer total reliability to our clients and we want reliability in return. For us, giving up reliability for glamour would be a bad trade off. Though it might make sense in terms of the skills of our company, staging rock concerts might not fit our image – and image matters to a company (or your local Lions club) as much as expertise. The two work together.

So celebrity management isn't what drives IMG.

Let's look even closer at who our clients are and what we do for them. They are world-class professionals – people who perform in Sydney as well as Los Angeles, in Paris as well as Tokyo. They are truly international figures. We find opportunities for them, trying to discover, and in some cases create, outlets for their talents.

So, finally, we have an accurate understanding of the central idea of IMG: it is a company that finds opportunities for top-notch professionals operating in the international arena. And that means:

1. If you don't have an accurate conception of your company's purpose, you tend to come up with tangential ideas that are obvious, but wrong.

2. If you have an accurate notion of your central purpose, you can come up with focused ideas that are fresh and right.

Knowing When to Say 'Yes' or 'No' to a Good Idea

Being in favour of good ideas is like being in favour of Mom and the flag. It's not going to get you into any arguments.

But there is a tendency to believe that *more* good ideas are *more* desirable. Because they feel that every good idea should be followed up, companies and people sometimes diversify more than they should.

If human energy was limitless, and if people's capacity for organization was infinite, wide diversification would make sense. In actual fact, following up on Idea B almost always takes attention and care away from Idea A – and sometimes the trade-off simply isn't worth it.

There are two situations in which it makes sense to pursue an idea outside your central idea: (1) when the market for your central idea is saturated; and (2) when you find yourself with tough competition in your basic business and can slide over into a related arena where there is less – or no – competition.

Let's say you're a baker. You've opened a shop in a town of a thousand families, and all you bake is bread. The first month you're in business, you sell, on average, one hundred loaves a day. In other words, you're reaching 10% of your prospective market.

But your bread is pretty good. It is much better than the packaged stuff that people are used to buying at the supermarket, and word starts to spread. So in your second month, you sell one hundred and fifty loaves a day. By the third month, you're near two hundred.

At this point you get a new idea: maybe you should start baking chocolate chip cookies. I would argue that baking chocolate chip cookies is probably a bad idea.

Your bread market is still growing – and, more important, it still has a long way to grow. Presumably, it is the quality of your bread that makes it sell; presumably, too, the quality would suffer somewhat if you started to divide your time and concentration between bread and cookies.

Remember, 80% of your prospective market is not yet buying your bread, and it's word of mouth that's expanding your sales. The last thing you need is for people to start saying, 'Joe's bread has gone downhill since he started baking cookies.'

In other words, you don't want to compromise the execution of your first idea just so you can try out another idea.

But let's say the situation is different. Let's say you're selling six hundred loaves a day. Well, now your market is nearing the saturation point. Word of mouth probably has done as much for you as possible. So, unless you are content to sit there and sell your six hundred loaves – and staying still is almost never a good idea – now is the time to expand into cookies.

This is not to say that it's now OK to let the quality of your bread go downhill; that is never OK. It is simply that the risks and benefits have shifted.

Let's say your bread business falls off by 10%, but within a few months you're selling 50% as much in cookies as in bread; that is a net gain of 40% to your business.

The other situation that might force you into diversification would be if another baker opened up in town. You might be the best breadmaker in five hundred miles, but human nature is funny and there is no accounting for taste: a certain proportion

142

of your market is going to defect. This always happens, in every field.

Whatever the relative quality of products or services, some customers and clients will always go to the other guy just because he *is* the other guy!

In this situation it is clearly a good idea for you to offer something the competition isn't offering. The customer's choice is now weighted in your favour: she can go to the other fellow for bread, or she can come to you for bread *and* cookies. Given comparable quality, people prefer one-stop shopping. But maintaining comparable quality is easier said than done.

If your first idea is working well and still has growth potential, think long and hard before you start chasing other ideas.

The First One There Doesn't Always Win

There is a tendency to believe that the first person to have an idea wins the race, gets the glory and reaps the benefits. In practice, this is very often not the case.

Consider the visionary developer who looks at a swamp and imagines a luxurious resort. He drains the swamp and clears the land, which takes a lot of time and costs a great deal of money. He has yet to turn a profit and his debt obligations are staggering. He is just about to dig the first foundation when his partners get tired of waiting and pull the plug.

So the visionary developer, the person who first had the idea, has no choice but to give up, and he's lucky if he covers his debts.

Enter Developer Two, the second person to have the idea. He looks at the prospective resort and he no longer sees swamp and virgin forest; he sees drained, cleared land that can be picked up at a reasonable price. So he buys the property.

But he has troubles of his own. He has to put together a workforce to build the place. He's got to find water. He's got to bring in power and lay roads. All this is costing him oodles of cash and, like the first fellow, he has yet to make an entry on the credit side of the ledger.

Let's say this second developer gets as far as printing up one of those glossy brochures with artists' impressions that make the half-finished resort look like a re-creation of the Garden of Eden. You've got your palm trees, your golf course, your sunset views – the works. (You don't see the drainage ditches, the 'lawns' where the sod has yet to take, the mosquitoes.) Now, a pretty hefty price tag has to be attached to those condominiums or time-shares, for a couple of reasons: a big investment has to be recouped and the developer – who really pictures his resort *as* the brochure – is determined to position his property as exclusive, high-end real estate.

Developer Two meets unexpected resistance on the marketing end. The buying public is less than eager to pay top-dollar for a half-finished resort in a place they've never heard of, much less seen written up in a slick magazine. Months drag on, creditors dun for payment and Developer Two bails out.

Along comes Developer Three – the one who is destined to cash in on the idea of the new resort. He pays a forced-sale price for the already improved real estate. He inherits a situation where at least some public awareness has been created. With the money he hasn't spent on clearing and draining, building and paving, he can launch a major marketing effort. He can advertise, and he can woo the sort of prestigious guests who are certain to attract others. The chances are that he'll do very well indeed.

The moral of the story?

The originator of an excellent idea is not guaranteed the fruits of his genius.

Timing as Part of Execution

Timing is an integral part of an idea. The *when* of an idea is inseparable from the *what* and the *how* of it.

Unlike many other aspects of executing an idea, timing is not an organizational or mechanical issue; it is an intuitive one. Since there will always be risks you can't avoid, you have got to be that much savvier in dodging those you can. There will be thrills enough without taking extra chances!

On more occasions than I care to remember, I have seen fundamentally sound, well-executed ideas come to nothing simply because they were inauspiciously timed. Sometimes an idea is good, the execution is world-class, and the airplane just doesn't fly. Or doesn't fly just then. It may very well fly at some time in the future.

I stress this because people have an understandable tendency to wash their hands and walk away from an idea that doesn't work. Up to a point, this tendency makes good sense. No one, after all, wants to keep throwing money at a hopeless cause. Equally important, no one wants to get obsessed with a project whose failure was cause for disappointment and depression. You've got to move on.

At the same time, however, it pays to keep a hand in if at all possible. This doesn't mean that you should pour good money after bad. Nor does it mean that you should neglect the other sides of life. But you should allow yourself a way back in, in case conditions become more auspicious.

Put the idea on the back burner, but don't lose sight of it. Keep a weather eye on the market and from time to time update your plans. If the moment comes, you may have to act fast – and unless you are ready in your own mind the moment will slip away from you.

The only thing more frustrating than having a good idea the public isn't ready for is losing the idea by the time the public does get ready!

CHAPTER EIGHT

Concepts and Misconceptions

Forming creative ideas is one of the great sacred mysteries. But the process of recognizing and implementing good ideas is a skill to be learned and a valuable application in all walks of life.

Your ideas will be tested in the context of other ideas. Inevitably, there will be questions of turf. There may be conflicting claims of originality. And there can be highly political squabbles as to who deserves credit for what.

Sometimes explaining and expediting your ideas just isn't enough; you have to fight for them. Coming up with an original new concept is less difficult than selling it to colleagues who may be jealous and superiors who may be threatened by change.

Human nature being what it is, most people tend to be overly fond of their own ideas. People see the good points in their schemes and overlook the drawbacks. They are indulgent of their ideas just as they are indulgent of their kids.

All of us have marvelled at someone else's good idea – it seems so obvious in retrospect. Why didn't *I* think of that? Instead of kicking yourself, put professional jealousy aside, sit down and figure out how that new concept works and why. In other words, go to school on it. Even though you may derive no direct benefit, you will be better equipped to sift the wheat from the chaff when developing your own ideas in the future.

Getting an idea is an intuitive process; understanding an idea is an intellectual process. The two are distinct.

It is a valuable distinction to learn. Not infrequently, for example, inventors can't see the applications of their handiwork. They may be geniuses, but they don't know exactly what it is they've done. Often it is a competitor who figures out the implications of the idea, lines up the financing and retools the factory.

Your competitors' ideas can help you if you use them as a springboard to take your own efforts higher – turning an extra somersault or twist to stay a step ahead.

The Elusive Win-Win Ideal

The best and most durable ideas are not the ones that allow you to profit at the expense of others, but the ones that allow everybody to benefit.

I stress this because I think many people have a tendency to view business – and human conduct generally – as a sort of *us* versus *them* affair. For our side to prosper, there must be someone else who's going down the tubes.

There is a lot of aggressiveness and conflict implicit in this view of the world. It makes for good stories in the business press, but it is not the way things really work.

Sure, you want to out-think, out-perform and out-manoeuvre your rivals. To that extent, business is a scrap. But you really fight the competition not head-to-head but by making yourself more worthy of your customer's trust.

Say IMG has a new business venture in mind. If we start thinking that the object is to cut up the other fellow, we are just wasting time and energy, distracting ourselves from the business at hand. The real business is to frame the idea in such a way that it doesn't work only for us but for everybody down the line.

Ideas have more than one constituency. The idea that serves one party well and others badly is usually poor for business.

147

The Mother of Invention

The question 'Whose Baby Is This?' troubles every organization. It makes junior people paranoid as they fret about whether their immediate superiors are taking credit for their original thinking.

It creates major headaches for heads of departments, who generally realize how far short they fall of Solomonic wisdom when it comes to judging between the competing claims of on-the-make subordinates.

It gives nightmares to CEOs, who realize that, not infrequently, contending factions would let the baby be cut in half sooner than give the other guy fair credit.

I wouldn't even venture to guess the number of good ideas that are scuttled, not because they are flawed or can't be implemented, but because they are subverted by people protecting their turf or denying credit to others.

Here is a classic illustration of a disillusioning experience: a spunky woman claims her MBA and goes to work at an advertising agency as an assistant account executive. She has a great theoretical understanding of how advertising works and how consumers should be wooed. What she doesn't seem to understand is how vulnerable she is to having her ideas appropriated by her boss.

He has been in the business half a dozen years. He is not an evil person. He doesn't necessarily mean to rip her off; maybe he is not even aware that he's doing it. But he is past the first flush of enthusiasm for his job. If he doesn't get a promotion soon with fresh responsibilities, he's going to go very stale. In order to hurry that promotion along, he is not above presenting some of his young assistant's clever notions as his own.

On learning that he has, she is enraged – and discouraged from putting forth her best efforts. She sulks, which hurts both the agency and her own chances of recognition.

Let's consider this destructive process and how it could be prevented or minimized. The chances are that in the normal course of the workday the account executive and the assistant have various opportunities to talk. Sometimes they talk in the

148

presence of others and sometimes they talk one-on-one. Which leads me to this advice:

There are two ways to safeguard your ideas: Tell nothing to anybody. Or tell everything to everybody.

In theory, either strategy will save you from getting ripped off. If no one hears your thoughts, then obviously you are safe. If you sing your ideas from the rooftops, probably no one will have the gall to claim them later as his own.

Both the No Disclosure and the Full Disclosure tactics need to be applied with great sensitivity. A subordinate, after all, can't simply refuse to talk to the boss. Then again, there is no rule to say that a subordinate has to have his or her brightest ideas in one-on-one situations.

Realistically, there will be one-on-one exchanges, and there is no such thing as an absolute assurance that some of your insights won't be misappropriated. That comes under the rubric paying dues, and anyone who avoids it altogether is probably leading a charmed life.

But save your pet ideas for larger meetings – for opportunities when you can impress people two or three levels up and when you will get full credit. Later you can always smile, and say: 'Gee, I guess I just think better in group situations.'

The View from the Top

An insecure executive may steal an idea from a naive assistant. A department head, out of absentmindedness or malice, may distribute credit unfairly. But the CEO – or person heading any organization, no matter its size – must create a structure in which ideas are encouraged and credit is duly given. He or she must set a tone that generates originality and the willingness to take calculated risks.

If the CEO allows the ideas of junior executives to be routinely misappropriated by their bosses, then the most creative and promising people will be angry – and they will leave the organization. The company will have found a brilliant way of ridding itself of top-notch people and building a staff of second-raters.

The kinds of incentives that get results vary, but the need for incentives is universal. The simple truth is that it is easier not to have ideas than to have them. It is easier not to express ideas than to go out on a limb by presenting them, thereby exposing the quality of one's mind. People need to be coaxed, and that's where incentives come in.

Commissions are the simplest and one of the commonest sorts of incentive. They work well in many situations but have drawbacks, too. They discourage teamwork since, in the typical instance, only one person gets the commission. They drain energy away from those parts of the job that don't lead directly to a payoff but still matter in terms of overall performance.

I prefer a structure of incentives – generally in the form of raises, promotions and occasionally bonuses – geared to an employee's contribution during the year.

I recognize specific ideas, sure, but I also look for a track record of innovative thinking. Equally important, I try to reward not only the originator of an idea but also the people who refine and implement it. As in basketball, I keep a place on my scorecard for the guy who makes the assist as well as the person who puts the ball through the net. If you reward only the employee who had the idea, you invite others to subvert it or, at the least, downplay it. Why should they do anything to help it along? If you reward idea-support as well as idea-origination, you welcome people into the creative process. This is something the Japanese do well.

Nothing is easier for a CEO or boss than to hide in his office and have almost no contact with anyone outside the small circle of his senior executives. These people, in most cases, will be near-contemporaries of the CEO. There is an easy rapport. And few names to remember.

Failing to trace the sources of good ideas from every level of his company is one of the biggest mistakes a CEO can make. If I don't talk to the people two levels down, how can I be sure that I am getting the full story from people one level down? How can I maximize the use of incentives unless I am aware that ideas are being buffered by several management levels before I even hear about them?

Jackie Stewart on 110% Awareness

I met Jackie Stewart more than twenty years ago, before he became World Champion three times on the Grand Prix racing circuit. Jackie wants more out of this life than anyone I know. In that sense, he is the epitome of the 110% achiever. He excels at everything he does, whether it is clay pigeon shooting or business or racing cars. You can attribute some of it to talent, some of it to a razor-sharp intellect, some of it to a keen sense of people.

It was not until I was forty-two years of age that I was identified as being dyslexic. That was a weight lifted off my shoulders. I thought, my God, I'm not stupid after all. I'm not thick. I'm not all those things people call me.

This awareness was the light of my life in a funny sort of way. I didn't care any more that I couldn't spell, or that I was a slow reader, or that to this day I do not know the letters of the alphabet, the words to the Lord's Prayer or the words to my own National Anthem, which I stood for so many times. That doesn't embarrass me any more.

Sitting in an airplane on a long journey, if I am writing a letter by hand, now I don't mind turning to ask the person in the seat next to me, 'How do you spell "what"?' They go home and say, 'You'll never believe this. Jackie Stewart can't spell "what"!' But that doesn't matter any more.

As a boy I just couldn't consume information. You get the mickey taken out of you, you get laughed at, you get sniggered at; somebody asks you to stand up and read a passage from a book, and you fumble and cough, and then everybody else starts coughing and sniggering. Some children become severely handicapped by dyslexia. They get chips on their shoulders. They get problems.

151

I was lucky. God gave me a pair of hands to hold a steering wheel. Had it not been for that I might have been a lost person. I might never have reached my true potential; lots of people don't, though in some way they could be great, they could be titans.

I left school at fifteen, not being good at anything. I worked in a garage, and I worked very hard to serve more petrol more quickly, to pump the tyres up and clean the windscreens and fill the radiator because I wanted to demonstrate that I could do it more quickly than anyone else. I didn't mind that it was a menial task, nor did I care about other people's views. Everybody said you're not going to get a Ph.D. for that. As far as I was concerned, I was getting a Ph.D. because I was doing it better than anyone else.

People were tipping me; they must have been pleased with the performance. That was my barometer. I was getting rewarded by gratuities and by verbal praise. The lubrication bays – I could have eaten my breakfast off any part of them – were where I displayed my skill over everybody else. I had the best lubrication bays in the county of Dumbarton. Until then, all I had was abuse, not from my parents, but from people generally.

I was so pleased to be doing well and getting praise for it that I continued to wish to do well. I never lost the thought that you have to give good value for the things you are paid for, and to try harder for the things you want to achieve to reach your ultimate limits.

People get confused about being competitive. All I'm interested in is doing things to the best of my ability. When you do that, you are your own greatest critic. You are not competing with another person, or against another person's weaknesses – other people's blunders are easy meat. If you have high standards of your own for achievement, you are a greater taskmaster. Your perception of excellence is your best judge. And you need 110% in order to execute that.

Around the time I left school I began to compete in clay pigeon meets. I won the first I entered on New Year's Day. Now, of course, I'm willing to accept that most Scotsmen on

152

New Year's Day are just slightly the worse for wear. And I was there fresh as a daisy at the age of fourteen and a half. I won an enormous trophy, which gave me great satisfaction. That was when I was bitten by the bug of competition. Later I learned how to be beaten with some humility and that I had to put a 110% effort into something to get anything back from it.

My best race, technically, was at Monza in 1973. That was a 110% effort – and I finished fourth.

You have to be clinical when you drive at the highest level, in fact when you do anything at that level. The biggest risk – in business, sport, life – is to allow your heart to rule your head. Your heart takes you in a direction that is quite often wrong. Your head has to be very clear.

On that day at Monza, I drove with as good a degree of accuracy as I think I ever have. I had a puncture on the seventh lap or something and it took a long time to change the wheel. The nuts wouldn't come off and I was left with a great deficit to make up. But I drove very precisely. It was an easy track. And if you drive very well, it is more difficult on an easy track than a difficult one where your virtuosity, your God-given skill, can be used to good effect.

That was the year – 1973 – when I realized suddenly that I couldn't take it any more. It sounds silly. Here I was living a jet-set life, colourful, glamorous, lots of money, great friends. I was still winning. But I had burned out. I was getting more aggravation than satisfaction. I suddenly thought, 'What am I doing? Do I really want to do this for the rest of my life?'

There is a point in everybody's life when you have to stop the bus and take a look at where you're going. There is a point beyond which you cannot keep improving. Nobody does.

I knew there were other things I wanted to do – so why hold on to an old raft when you can build a speedboat? [Since leaving Formula One, Jackie has developed management and consulting relationships with organizations such as Goodyear, Ford, Rolex and British Telecom. He has also launched Paul Stewart Racing, which is not only a successful Formula One racing team but is designed as an incubator for up-and-coming drivers.] Through the years I continue to learn. I feel that every day is new, that I'm going to enjoy it and bring myself up in terms of knowledge and awareness. I know I'm better now than I was, say, two years ago – better at applying myself, thinking things out, using my skills positively.

Many businessmen I meet have egos because they have never been acknowledged. They are big fish in a small pond. Too many chairmen or executive vice-presidents have a corporate strut – they'll never walk anywhere without two or three people with them. They have to have the padding of that 'comfort blanket' of yes-men. I'm always suspicious of people who have to travel in groups and have entourages – people who are not prepared to have dinner or go to the cinema on their own. They have no personal confidence in their own skill or ability or presence. So many people need to have 'position'. That isn't what getting 110% from life is about.

The 111% Non-Solution

Too much of a good thing is too much.

I mention this not to contradict myself in a book extolling the virtues of maximizing your time, talents and opportunities, but rather to point out the obvious caveat: trying too hard can be as bad as not trying hard enough.

In my ideal world, each of us would have an internal meter telling us what constitutes good, excellent or extraordinary effort. Alarms would go off when we were giving less than our best.

Likewise, alarms would go off when we were giving too much, when we went over the line from 110% to 111% effort. The meter would warn us when we were overworked, when the risks of doing something outweighed the potential reward of achieving it, when we were asking too high a price or expecting too much in a deal. Like Jackie Stewart, we should learn how to pace ourselves to maintain that edge of precision.

The 111% problem comes in all shapes and sizes, but the results are invariably damaging – to your talent, performance, reputation and well-being.

The most obvious examples come from sports.

The athlete who overtrains, who pushes his body further than it can go, is guilty of giving 111%. He invariably pays the price in the form of an injury that stops him from training altogether. Net result: he is further back than when he started.

So is the golfer who tries to drive the ball too far. More often than not, he walks to the tee pumped up with adrenalin and ready to swing as hard as he can. What follows is not a pretty sight. His form deteriorates. He abandons the natural mechanics of a good swing, loses his physical poise – and rarely ends up in the fairway.

True champions do the opposite. They walk up to the ball reminding themselves to relax, to bring the club back slowly, to maintain their alignment. If all goes well and they *don't* exert themselves unnaturally, they will hit the ball as far as they usually do – and with a friendly breeze or the right bounce, maybe 10% farther.

The parallels outside sports are less obvious but infinitely more numerous. You see the dangers of 111% in:

- The boss who overcontrols his employees and is always telling them what to do. At some point, they will tune him out – and he has lost their respect.

- The salesman who pesters his customers for orders and ends up irritating rather than persuading them.

- The negotiator who wants to squeeze the last dollar out of every deal and ends up poisoning a relationship at the moment it should be flourishing.

- The neighbour who tries too hard to impress you with his home, his hobbies, his vacations, his gadgets – but who leaves you quite unimpressed with his personality.

155

- The hostess who works so hard preparing a meal for her guests that she is too busy or too exhausted to enjoy the party with them.

- The friend who praises you indiscriminately when candour would be the better course.

No one is immune from going too far. The line between an extraordinary effort and an excessive one is extremely fine. Even the best of us, with the best intentions, overstep it.

Jimmy Carter's last year as President is a painful example. Carter became so consumed by the hostage crisis in Iran that it paralysed his administration. He devoted all his energy to seeking the release of the hostages, to 'micromanaging' every detail, even though there was little he could do. His intentions may have been noble, but he went too far. The more he tried, the more frustrated and powerless he appeared. In effect, he became a hostage in the White House, and it probably cost him the next election.

How do you protect yourself from the 111% non-solution, especially when everything around you (including this book) reminds you that you should always be moving forward, trying harder, doing more? How do you recognize when you have gone, as the British say, 'over the top'? Some points to consider:

1. Beware the Single idea

As the French philosopher Emile Chartier said, 'Nothing is more dangerous than an idea when it is the only one you have.'

To become fixated on a single idea, on one point of view, on one way of doing something, is probably the easiest trap to fall into – and perhaps the biggest reason people go over the 110% line.

There are virtues to having tunnel vision, especially when it inspires you to keep going where lesser mortals would have quit, but not if it comes at the expense of good judgement and good results.

156

A few years ago, when Jack Tucker took over the Arnold Palmer Golf Company from a flamboyant, free-spending executive, one of his first official acts was to sell the company plane and hang the keys on his office wall. When people asked about the keys, Tucker would proudly say, 'We sold the plane'. To him the keys were a powerful symbol, a reminder of the company's previous profligate ways.

This gesture might have worked, but Tucker carried his philosophy too far. He went overboard on austerity. He was so keen on slashing costs that he lost sight of the company's marketing needs. He failed to maximize Arnold Palmer's name. He took the company from one extreme to another. Now it was boring, unaggressive and because of drastic cost-cutting not as profitable as it should have been.

2. Learn to say No

If you become adept at saying No, you will rarely be overcommitted or overextended.

You will rarely have to break a promise.

You will rarely have to compromise.

You will never burn out.

You will be able to give 110% on your terms, not someone else's.

You will function at your best and have a little left in reserve.

We had a salesman in our corporate marketing group who simply could not say No. In meetings to decide who would call on specific companies, he was always raising his hand, saying, 'I'll take that one'. His files bulged with prospects. The funny thing was, he could sell when he gave himself enough time to do the job properly. But he spread himself too thin.

He ended up doing the company and himself a disservice. The sales he made couldn't erase all the opportunities that fell through the cracks. He would have been much better off saying No. By taking on less work, he would have accomplished much more.

157

3. Cut corners – but carefully

There is nothing wrong with taking a short cut on occasion. I admire people who can speed up a project or simplify a procedure by cleverly economizing on time and effort. But again, it is easy to take this too far.

If someone in our company can break through to a decision-maker by avoiding the decision-maker's deputies and gate-keepers, I congratulate them. But I would certainly have second thoughts if the gambit significantly irritated those deputies and gatekeepers. After all, we will want to get through those gates a lot more times in the future and gatekeepers have long memories.

Cut too many corners and people will conclude that taking shortcuts is the only way you do business. No one really likes a sneak or cheat, no matter how clever or daring he may be. It comes back to haunt you.

A man who had been my son Todd's classmate at Duke University once contacted me about a job at our company. I asked Todd about him. Todd said, 'I'm not sure if you ought to meet him or not. Let me tell you this story and you decide.'

It seems that, in order to graduate from Duke, the young man had to write a major paper for a psychology professor. For whatever reason, the student kept putting off the paper. He got so wrapped up in graduation activities that finally he didn't have time to write it.

The deadline passed. The professor announced the grades – and failed the young man.

The student confronted the professor. 'Why did I flunk?' he asked.

'You didn't turn in the paper,' said the professor. 'What!' the young man exclaimed. 'I spent nine weeks writing the best paper I've ever written at this school for your course. And you lost it!'

Ultimately, he convinced the professor to change the grade.

There are places in the business world for someone with that much nerve, but not at our company. I decided not to meet him.

4. Don't run up the score

Another insidious aspect of giving 111% is how it can skew your perspective on what really matters in life. You get so focused on achieving your own objectives that you forget the other side has objectives too.

In most sports, being sensitive to your opponent isn't a big issue. In tennis, if you have your opponent on the ropes, you had better put him away. You don't want to let him back in the match. But even in sports you never want to humiliate an opponent. All too often, you will rue the day you did it.

The dynamic is different in a business negotiation (and most other forms of human interaction). Having the upper hand in sports is a weapon, and you are expected to use it. In business, having the upper hand is a responsibility, and you are often ahead of the game when you don't use it.

My friendship with Chris Lewinton, now the chairman of an international company, TI Group, was sealed back in 1961 because we *didn't* do business with each other. Lewinton was running Wilkinson Sword's US operations at the time and had committed $25,000 for some promotional activities with Arnold Palmer. However, before the promotion hit full stride, the bottom fell out of Wilkinson's profit projections. Lewinton was ordered to make drastic cuts.

One of the cuts, naturally, was the Palmer promotion. But we had a signed agreement.

(In other words, I had the upper hand.)

We met, he explained the altered climate at Wilkinson and asked if we were willing to defer the deal to a later date. He also mentioned that if I insisted on holding him to the agreement, he would come up with the $25,000, which was not an insignificant sum back then.

(In other words, not only did I have the upper hand, but he was willing to let me play it out.)

Without hesitating, I told him not to worry about it.

That turned out to be a very smart decision, though I didn't know it at the time. We never did resume the Palmer promotion.

In fact, Lewinton and I didn't meet again for several years. But since the late 1960s, our respective companies have done considerable business together. As for Chris Lewinton, he has become a trusted adviser and friend.

In hindsight and as I write this, letting Lewinton off the hook seems like an obvious decision: lose a customer in the short term, gain a friend for life. But most decisions of this kind are not at all clear when you make them.

How would you respond in a similar situation? You have closed a sale, reported it to your superiors and practically spent the money. When all the facts confirm that you have the advantage, when every fibre of your being tells you to charge ahead, when even the other party admits that you are well within your rights to stick to an agreement, would you have the discipline to take the short-term hit with no guarantee of a long-term payoff?

That is a 110% question. Be honest with yourself – and you'll find the 110% answer.

The Extraordinary Power of the Extraordinary Gesture

Most of us, by upbringing or inclination, are not trained to make the grand or eccentric gesture. But travelling a long distance to call on a customer or devoting an inordinate amount of time to one individual can have benefits that far exceed the effort we put into them. In that sense, they are 110% efficient.

Extraordinary gestures, in fact, don't have to be particularly extraordinary, just a notch above what is expected.

I once called on Jack Murray, the then owner and chairman of Prince Racquets, at his headquarters in Princeton, New Jersey. This wasn't a particularly onerous task. Jack is a wonderful person and Princeton is only a ninety-minute drive from our Manhattan office. But he told me that my visit meant a lot to him because none of the other people we were competing with in tennis at the time had taken the trouble to do that.

Another time I happened to be in Australia when we were

concluding an arrangement to sell some of Arnold Palmer's companies to NBC. I flew to New York to complete the deal and flew right back to Australia. I think that affected the NBC people and helped push them to wrap up the agreement. I know this is how I feel when people travel a long way to see me. I often wish they hadn't made the effort because it makes me feel obliged to them, which may not always be in my client's best interest or mine.

Never say, 'Let's have lunch' – unless you mean it

I've always thought that following up on a promise or invitation is one of the more extraordinary gestures in modern social relations – because it is so rare.

All of us make empty social promises.

'Let's have lunch' and 'We must get together soon' are among the most insincere statements in the English language. People use them as throwaway sentences, like 'Good morning' or 'Goodbye'. Quite often, both sides of that dialogue know how empty the invitation really is.

I try to make my invitations as genuine as possible. If someone mentions that they will be in England in June or July, my reflex response is, 'If you're there during Wimbledon, give me a call. Be my guest for the day.' (That is a 50% solution to the information that our social schedules may intersect. Like everyone else, I'm trying to be polite.)

Now, the odds are that that individual won't be there during Wimbledon. Even if he is, given the insincerity most of us factor into such casual invitations, he probably won't give me a call.

But what if I follow up a week or two later with a letter confirming my invitation? I say, in effect, 'You mentioned you would be in England. I want you to know that the best Wimbledon dates are from 26 June to 3 July. If you give me a little notice, I'll make sure we can get together.' (That's a 75%

161

solution. I've added some meaning and substance to an otherwise empty gesture.)

The next step is where I part company with some people.

If I don't hear from this gentleman in a reasonable amount of time, I remind him again. Either my secretary or I will call his office, mention my letter and politely enquire about his travel plans.

(That is my 110% solution. Not only have I demonstrated my sincerity, but without being pushy or overbearing I have forced him to acknowledge it. I get credit for being a generous and efficient fellow – whether he accepts my invitation or not.)

Never shrink your Christmas card list

Continuing gestures are an interesting variation on the extra-ordinary gesture.

Continuing gestures are those small, thoughtful touches you do for friends and business acquaintances that are dictated by the calendar – sending them a card each Christmas, inviting them to your vacation home at least once each summer, renewing their gift subscription to the *Economist* or buying them a drink on their birthday. The fact that you remember is more impressive than the gesture itself.

The trouble with continuing gestures, of course, is that you cannot discontinue them without a good reason.

Buzzer Hadingham, the former chairman of the All England Lawn Tennis and Croquet Club, says that the first time he invites someone to sit in the Royal Box at Wimbledon, they love it. But some people, heedless that invitations are limited, expect to be invited again year after year. The disappointment created the year they aren't invited virtually cancels out all the goodwill generated by inviting them in the first place.

This sort of thing can reach comic proportions. For years I've sent gourmet popcorn and cookies to a long list of friends at Christmas. I once had the chairman of a major corporation needling me because one year he didn't receive the cookies. It wasn't that he missed the cookies. But he was curious about the change.

That is why you should never shrink your Christmas card list. The people who no longer receive your Season's Greetings will always wonder why you stopped. Understandably.

Just say 'I'm sorry'

Apologizing to friends when we have disappointed them is also one of those rare gestures.

There are a lot of people in this world who are constitutionally incapable of saying 'I'm sorry'. Perhaps they like to put their failures behind them as quickly as possible. Perhaps they can't admit they were wrong.

I suspect, however, that the inability to own up to a mistake and apologize, which is easy to do, strains and destroys relationships more often than any other personal failing.

In a way it's like lending money to a friend. It is common wisdom that if you lend money to a friend and expect the friendship to last, don't expect to be paid back.

But at some point, if the friend can't pay you back, you will at least expect him to mention it. Quite often, the acknowledgement is just as valuable as the actual repayment of the debt.

A few years ago I had dinner in London with a businessman who, after a meteoric rise, had run into hard times. On his way up he had asked our company to do many things for him. We went out on a lot of limbs for him with clients, customers and sports federations. But his financial problems left us high and dry. A lot of our promises and obligations fell apart because of him, and I was the one who had to go back to our clients and explain it to them.

These things happen, despite our best intentions. I can accept that.

But over our dinner, to my surprise, he acted as if nothing had happened. He talked about his bad luck with interest rates and how he was stabbed in the back by labour unions.

If at some point during dinner he had acknowledged the

163

compromising position he had put me in – if he had said, 'I'm sorry, Mark, I realize you stuck your neck out for me and this has to be embarrassing for you' – I could have dealt with all his problems. But he didn't, for which he went down immeasurably in my esteem.

Don't confuse by extravagance

Extraordinary gestures don't have to be extravagant. On the contrary, I think extravagance can confuse a relationship. Suddenly, the person on the receiving end has a feeling of 'I owe you one' that he perhaps cannot repay. There is a reason so many people respond to a surprisingly lavish gift by exclaiming, 'Oh, you shouldn't have!' Quite often, they really mean it.

The best gestures are timed well, or add a special touch, or display a level of insight and caring that works far better than extravagance.

Stanley Marcus, the founder of the Nieman-Marcus department stores and an authority on extraordinary gestures, says his favourite gift was receiving eighty Hermĕs ties from the chairman of Hermĕs on his eightieth birthday. Now that *was* extravagance but what tickled Marcus was the wonderful simplicity of the idea. A tie as a present (even a Hermĕs tie) is something of a cliché. But one for each year of your life makes the gift memorable.

I was once taken to dinner by a friend and we got around to talking golf. As we tried to top one another with tales of our play, he mentioned that he had lost thirteen golf balls during a round the week before. A few days later I sent him a thank-you note for dinner, together with thirteen golf balls. Remembering the specific number and replacing his losses was a small gesture, perhaps. But it was one he never forgot.

Even the most curmudgeonly among us have this talent. We are all capable of unusual thoughtfulness when our parents have a major anniversary or someone we love has a significant birthday (i.e., one with a zero attached to it). Those are the occasions when we pull out all the stops, when we exceed ourselves in terms of effort and creativity. Milestones matter.

Well, perhaps we should try to treat every day, every meeting, every conversation as something like a potential milestone.

If you can tap into that wellspring of sensitivity to people on a daily basis, the rewards might not be immediate or obvious. But thoughtful gestures for friends and colleagues are like putting money in the bank and earning compound interest on it. Over time, you will end up as the richest person in town.

CHAPTER NINE

Reaping the Most from Your Opportunities

One of the unkindest stereotypes America has ever produced is the Salesman: the hectic, perspiring, fast-talking man who stops at nothing to clinch a sale. This inaccurate stereotype doesn't reflect badly only on the men and women who actually earn their livings in sales. It reflects badly on all of us.

For all of us, in various ways, sometimes direct, sometimes oblique, are salesmen.

We have things we offer others, things we hope others can be persuaded to accept. Our offerings might be market-place commodities – widgets, services, entertainment. Or a certain vision of ourselves, an overture towards friendship, even a promise of love. The medium of exchange for our offerings might be money – but it could also be respect, professional regard, even affection. The point is that the art of persuasion is used across the whole spectrum of human experience.

Persuasion and Manipulation

Persuasion and manipulation are quite different things. I stress this because there are some who see life as one big battlefield; they argue that when you try to convince anyone of anything, you're manipulating him. That simply is not so.

166

Persuasion is positive. When you want to persuade someone, you speak in terms of benefits. You offer value, beauty, profits, happiness. You plug into what the other person desires.

Manipulation is negative. When you want to manipulate someone, you speak in terms of consequences. The operative device is the veiled threat. You plug not into what the other person wants, but into what he fears.

Let me give an illustration:

An encyclopaedia salesman comes to your home. For openers, he tries to persuade you to buy the encyclopaedia. He tells you all the good things. He tells you about the 50,000 leading experts who've contributed articles. He shows you the quality of the printing. He runs his hand over the buckram bindings. He extols the virtues of the hardwood cabinet included free if you pay in cash. Now, if at this point you buy the encyclopaedia, fine – you've been persuaded, not manipulated.

But what if you don't? The chances are that the salesman looks over at your eight-year-old daughter and ten-year-old son and starts talking about how competitive it is to get into a good college. If kids don't write good term papers in junior high, they don't get into the fast-track classes in high school. And unless they're near the tippy-top of their high-school class, well, you can kiss Harvard and Yale goodbye. So now the salesman is playing on your fears and your guilt.

The question is no longer, Do you want the encyclopaedia? The question has become, Are you ready to accept responsibility for ruining your children's lives? Are you such a beast that you'll sell your kids down the river rather than pay five lousy dollars a week?

This is manipulation, pure and simple – salesmanship at its most carnivorous and unpleasant.

Now, let's not be naive or disingenuous: there are certainly times when manipulation works, and many an encyclopaedia has been sold long after the positive sales pitch had failed and the salesman was reaching into the very bottom of his bag of tricks.

The point is to recognize that persuasion and manipulation,

167

being two distinct approaches, have very different consequences beyond the sale.

Typically, an encyclopaedia salesman will deal with you once. If the style of his sales pitch breeds anger and resentment, well, that's not very good in human terms, but in business terms, so what?

But can you imagine doing business with the same customer on that basis again? That is the pragmatic justification for steering clear of manipulative techniques and for relying on persuasive ones.

Persuasion builds relationships. Manipulation builds nothing but barriers.

Who Are You Talking To?

Different people – and different companies – have different needs. They have different histories, budgets, images, styles. The process of persuading them has to take those unique circumstances into account.

Yet I am constantly amazed to see how often people take a one-size-fits-all approach to persuasion. They have their pitch and they use it, period. Whether they're talking to Du Pont or to the guy who orders for the corner store. Whether they're talking to their assistant or to their kids.

Thinking Small

People like to be listened to, and hate *not* being listened to. Being listened to makes people feel important and gives them confidence that their particular situation and needs are being addressed.

To be an effective persuader, however, you must be a good listener – and make it clear that you are listening.

One way to do it is to make a suggestion dramatically illustrating that you are moving beyond the typical preconception of that person's or that company's needs. You are letting them know that you are paying very close attention to what they are trying to tell you.

Let me give an example:

In our business, as in most, there is a tendency to make the size of the deal proportional to the size of the company you're dealing with. If you're dealing with IBM, say, the typical assumption is that it would be interested in major sponsorship of a top-drawer event, and a price-tag of several million would not be a deterrent if there was value and prestige in the exposure.

There is nothing wrong with that preconception. It is correct more often than not. It is consistent with what the needs and approaches of major corporations usually are. Usually, but not always.

Sometimes a big company might get more benefit from a small deal. And if you're the salesman who proposes that, you too will benefit in several ways. The company will be grateful that you listened hard enough to come up with an original solution. Trust will be built by the fact that you're suggesting a deal that will cost them less than they probably expected. Because you offered them a smaller price tag this time, the chances are that they'll come to you for something with a bigger price tag next time.

The idea is not necessarily to make the biggest sale, but the smartest sale. The 110% solution is to make the *best* sale – best being defined as most effective in building a profitable long-term relationship.

The Trojan Horse Approach to Selling

As anyone who has ever sold anything knows, the hardest part is getting in the door. It means getting the physical and psychological access to someone so that doing business becomes possible.

That access is a valuable commodity. Sometimes you have to make a sacrifice to get it but the sacrifice can become a very wise investment. Doing a small, relationship-building deal when you might do a bigger, one-shot deal is a worthwhile sacrifice. Consider the deal you don't really want to do. It brings you little or no money. It costs you a lot of time and trouble. But it puts you in line for better things. It gets your number in the Rolodex, and often pays big dividends in the longer haul.

Let's say Joe is setting up shop as a stockbroker. A brokerage house gives him a desk, a telephone and an enormous list of names, and Joe diligently sets about the exhausting and humiliating process of making cold calls.

Ninety-five per cent of the people he calls dismiss him out of hand. Either they have got a broker, or they are just not interested, or they consider themselves too important to do business with a fellow starting out.

That leaves five per cent who are even willing to chat with Joe. But some of those people are just being polite, or are just passing the time. Say two per cent are, in fact, potential customers.

At least some of those people are going to pass, explaining 'Gee, the market's just too volatile for me right now and I'm just keeping my money on deposit.' So how about if Joe says, 'Then why don't you consider letting me handle your deposits for you. I'll do the research. I'll do the legwork. I'll guarantee you the highest interest rate. And it'll cost you nothing.' In the short term, this is a pain for Joe. He gets no commissions. He's got a lot of paperwork to do. It's not even interesting.

But think about the upside. When a cold call is over, it's over. But now Joe has a perfect pretext to call Mr Smith and talk about his money – rolling deposits over, fluctuating rates, anything. And when he calls, you can bet Mr Smith will pay close attention. He has got money invested, after all. More important, from Joe's perspective, the customer is getting to know this young man, to have some confidence in him. Mr Smith isn't stupid – he knows that Joe is providing a service and getting nothing in return. And, if Mr Smith is like the great majority of people, he'll have a conscience about it: he'll be inclined to let Joe reap some benefit down the road.

Let's say market volatility lessens, and Mr Smith does buy stock. Where do you think he'll go with his order? Or suppose that a friend of Mr Smith's asks him to recommend a broker: whose name will be on his mind? Joe isn't just doing business, he's building business. That's what Trojan Horse salesmanship is all about.

More Door-Openers

Consider the radical tactic of taking a loss on a piece of work. There is a calculated risk here, and it should be used sparingly. But let's remember our central subject in this part of the book: *Opportunities. Creating them. Recognizing them. Making the most of them.*

Sometimes, taking an early hit is worth it.

At IMG, when we come up with a new idea for a television sports show, we've got both a terrific opportunity and a difficult persuasion job on our hands. TV programming is a high-ticket item and television executives – whose jobs ride on their decisions – tend to be conservative. The further you go from things that have been done before, the greater your chances of really hitting it big – but the greater your chances, also, of falling on your face.

Very occasionally, therefore, to sell a new programme, we have agreed to take a loss on the pilot or on the first instalment. We've got a network to underwrite part of the idea and the rest we've done out-of-pocket, with no guarantee of getting the money back.

The disadvantages of this arrangement are obvious. But what are the advantages? For one thing, confidence is catching and if we say to the network, 'We have so much faith in this project that we'll go into hock to get it produced', then the chances are that the network will have faith in it as well.

For another thing, our agreeing to be partners-in-risk greatly bolsters the case that our network-contact can make to *his* company.

171

A very big part of selling is arming your apparent buyer with positive arguments that he can sell when he gets back to headquarters.

In many and perhaps most business situations, the person you're dealing with doesn't have authority to make an on-the-spot unilateral decision. He's got to present the proposition to his boss or to a committee. In the typical instance, the first person you spoke with will be the advocate or champion of the idea, and the others need to be persuaded. So you have to make an ally of the first guy. You have to give him the chance to look good. He may say, 'This is a very promising but unusual concept, and I managed to get IMG to agree to absorb some of the risk.'

Forget that *we* were the ones who offered to absorb the risk. Let your contact take the credit. It costs you nothing, and it stokes his enthusiasm.

Taking the Confrontation Out of Selling

Remember in old movies how the leading man would try to kiss the leading lady and the leading lady, no matter how much she wanted to be kissed, would offer firm and even stubborn resistance? This was the standard game. Even though a kiss was mutual – what could be more mutual, after all? – both sides still kept up the time-honoured charade that one party wanted the kiss, while the other did not. Thus, an oddly competitive situation was contrived. Until the kiss was granted, the woman was thought to be winning. The kiss itself sealed the victory of the man.

Well, if you substitute 'seller' for 'leading man', and if you substitute 'buyer' for 'leading lady', you can grasp something very basic – if illogical – about the nature of sales. At the emotional if not the intellectual level, a sale is still regarded as something of a conquest.

If I can get you to buy something from me, I've won. If you refuse to buy, you've defeated me.

No matter that the buyer might benefit as much as or more

than the seller. Emotionally, that just isn't the point. A selling situation nearly always contains an element of confrontation, and no one likes to back down. The buyer's knee-jerk impulse, therefore – no matter what the content of the deal – is to resist.

There are two approaches in dealing with this, and they are poles apart. You can take the confrontational element to the limit. This, frankly, is a technique I find abrasive and undignified – but for certain people in certain situations, it gets results.

When someone browbeats you into purchasing an extended service-contract on your new washer-dryer, that's confrontational. You probably don't feel that an extended contract is in your best interests, but the pain of spending the money is less than the pain of listening to an obnoxious salesperson.

This is selling as total war, and buying as total surrender, and I feel sorry for people who have to do business on that basis. They must be bruised and misanthropic by the end of the day.

A much better way of dealing with the confrontational element in selling is to try to downplay it, to turn the 'competition' into a collaboration.

Show Them Your Basket of Goodies

Before the advent of suburban shopping centres, bakery vans used to make the rounds of many neighbourhoods, selling their goods door to door. To do this, they employed a technique that I think has symbolic value in many kinds of sales.

The salesman had a big wire basket, and he'd load it up with samples of everything the bakery had – muffins, cupcakes, pies, you name it. He'd carry this basket of goodies to the door, and he'd simply show it to Mrs Jones. If the salesman had some personality, he'd exchange pleasantries and make general chit-chat; but he wouldn't say, 'Hey, Mrs Jones, I want you to buy an apple pie.'

No, he'd totally defuse the buyer-seller confrontation by quietly presenting his goods and encouraging the customer to

173

pick. The decision was hers. There was no pressure, and not even any advice – unless the advice was asked for.

The bakery-basket approach played off a basic element of human nature: show someone an array of baked goods (or of cars, stocks or dresses) and the appetite for buying something will be increased.

Say I am meeting with the CEO of a company which is a potential sponsor of IMG events – a company we have not done business with before. I know the CEO is interested in buying; otherwise there would be no meeting. I have no idea what he'd like to buy, or how much he'd like to spend. So I present my basket of goodies.

I don't say, 'Well, for $300,000, you can get this and that sort of exposure at the Australian Open.' The specific price-tag would set a confrontational tone. The specific mention of the Australian Open – or any particular event – would be a bad idea at that stage. The chances are that the CEO would immediately become suspicious: why is he pushing me in that direction? Why does he assume we want tennis? Maybe he's got a problem with another sponsor and he's just trying to slot us in for his own convenience.

Now, all these paranoid complications can be avoided by the bakery-basket approach. Of course, there is a danger that a potential customer will be overwhelmed with options – and a good salesperson has to have an intuitive sense of when to move from presenting possibilities to steering the customer towards a choice. But I stress that the 'steering' should be done after the bakery-basket has been lovingly examined. That way, the customer feels not manipulated, but assisted.

The Curse of the Sales Call

The sales call, by definition, is a confrontation. The buyer knows you're coming to get some of his money. He's braced for the assault. He's rehearsing the techniques he's learned for saying No. Since the sales call, typically, is conducted in the buyer's office or home, he's also got turf to protect.

For all these reasons, I advise salespeople, whenever possible, to do the selling outside the scheduled sales call. Do it on the golf course. Do it over lunch. Do it anywhere – *but not when you're facing off across a desk.*

The Even Bigger Curse of the Sales Meeting

Take the confrontation of a sales call, multiply it by a hundred, and you begin to understand what you're up against in a situation where there are several individuals on the buying side. These people will play to each other as much as, or more than, they will cogently address the business at hand.

No one will want to seem weak. No one will want to seem gullible. The upshot is that they'd rather let a good deal go by, in the name of being tough, than accept a good deal at the risk of seeming easy.

Probably the most that can be done with this sort of sales meeting is to throw out an idea and save the actual selling of it for a one-on-one meeting later.

It's Both What You Know and Who You Know

Talk about opportunities and you're talking, among other things, about contacts – who you know, how you know them, how much they'll be willing to help you along, and why. You're talking, in other words, about all the many ways your ambitions intersect with those of others.

Those who are very successful in business, or in any field, often play down the role filled by the people they've known and leaned on at various points during their rise to prominence. It's the rare person who will give others any more of the credit than he absolutely has to.

At the other extreme, those who fall short of their goals in life have a strong tendency to attribute the other fellow's success

175

purely and simply to 'whom he knows'. There may well be an element of truth in this. However, people who ascribe another's success to 'contacts' are protecting their egos.

Sure, having well-placed friends can give a person a head start – anybody who denies that is an ostrich. But contacts will take you only so far. They'll open doors; but once inside, you've got to perform.

Family favours are nice, old school loyalties are terrific, but . . .

The contacts that truly matter are the ones you make yourself. Your father's friend will help you once; your own friends will help you for a lifetime.

People will assist you in valuable ways if they believe that you are valuable – valuable not in the sense of a *quid pro quo*, but in the sense of pursuing a substantive achievement of your own. People will want to participate in your progress if you yourself show an enthusiasm for your own goals and purposes.

The best way to expand on who you know is to expand on what you know. People are always drawn to information. So keep some handy. Have something to say. Do that, and people will want to talk to you again.

A Pull Up the Ladder

There is a natural loyalty and *esprit* among people of a similar age. This loyalty is such a deep-seated part of human nature that it generally persists even among peers who seem to be head-to-head competitors.

The dynamic goes something like this: You and I may get mad at each other to gain an advantage day-to-day, but in our hearts we know we'll both do better as our generation gets its shot at running things.

This is the way of the world. Today's assistants are tomorrow's managers, today's subordinates are tomorrow's CEOs.

If you curry favour with your seniors at the expense of good relationships with your peers, you may be making a bad trade-off over time. Maybe a senior can do more for you today. But peers will be matching your progress every step of the way.

All Things Being Equal . . .

People would rather do business with someone they know and like than with someone they don't know.

Business, no matter how pragmatic, is still an interpersonal activity. The flavour of business is significantly affected by the personality of those you deal with. The mechanics of doing business are often eased on the strength of personal affinities. Being able to call someone at home if need be; knowing each other's style of expression so that things can be explained with five words rather than ten: these are among the advantages of dealing with someone you know.

There are many factors besides cost that go into deciding a business deal. And most of those – goodwill, chances for repeat business, prestige, image – simply cannot be quantified. Even in situations where it's obvious that all things aren't quite equal, people would still rather do business with their friends. Don't misunderstand me. People don't – or certainly shouldn't – make bad deals in the name of doing business with friends. No one but a fool or a felon gives away the store on the basis of a personal association.

The point is that even good deals contain large grey areas and offer considerable room for personal discretion.

Winning the Judgement Calls

How can you tip the balance so that people will choose to do business with you?

Always show concern

I have argued throughout this book that the efficient use of time is a crucial component of success, and all of us should strive to use our minutes better.

But there are true and false efficiencies. One of these false efficiencies is to be so hell-bent on getting business done that you never pause to put your dealings on a personal plane.

Maybe you begin a conversation with a lukewarm 'how are you?' – a question, by the way, that calls for a formulaic answer, an answer that's usually not listened to anyway. Beyond that grudging concession to good manners, where do you go? How do you show concern for the other person?

Failing to do this is not only rude, but it represents a missed opportunity of grand proportions. Maybe the person across the desk has kids the same age as yours. That constitutes a tremendous natural bond. But how will you know if you never ask about his or her family?

The personal element is not tangential to business. It is *business.*

Never assume your product sells itself

No matter how great your product is, it takes a human being to sell it. If people don't like talking to you, they'll find an incredible number of reasons not to pick up the phone.

Favours

When you do someone a favour, it is an advertisement for yourself. It shows what you're capable of. Think of it as an audition – and don't miss your cue.

But on the Other Hand . . .

There are certain times when one should avoid doing business with friends.

If a piece of business has a reasonable likelihood of turning adversarial, you're better off dealing with a stranger. In dealing with a friend, the chances are that in an adversarial situation you won't pursue your own advantage as vigorously as you should. And even if you don't take the gloves off and duke it out, you'll probably damage the friendship anyway.

Declining to do business with a friend is very difficult. But sometimes it is really the kindest thing to do. Not long ago, I had a house built in Central Florida. It so happens that a major client has a son-in-law who runs a successful construction company in Orlando, and I felt a strong inclination to do business with him. But I didn't.

Why? As anyone who has ever had a house built will testify, a million things can go wrong and a few thousand usually do. Whenever you have a house built, you've got to accept the possibility of ending up in court with your builder. And frankly, I didn't want personal loyalty to get in the way of my being truly difficult if I had to.

I don't accept the metaphor of business as war, or assertiveness as the key to success in human dealings. But I do recognize that sometimes things turn into a scrap. Loyalties don't exist so that we can 'use' them; they exist because they tap into a fundamental human need for caring. Friendship does not depend on mutual back-scratching but on real affinities and an ever-expanding base of shared experience.

Relationships built around the mechanics of *quid pro quo* tend to dissolve as soon as someone changes jobs or just gets tired of the game. Relationships based on respect and mutual curiosity are the ones that last.

179

CHAPTER TEN

The Gentle Art of Persuasion

For aeons philosophers have tried to define what distinguishes human beings from the rest of the animal kingdom. Some say what sets us apart is our ability to reason. Others that it is our use of language. And so on. I would like to offer another uniquely human attribute: Man is the only animal that negotiates.

When lions kill, the leader of the pride takes the prime bits while the others settle for leftovers. There's nothing for the lions to discuss. That's just the way it is. Only humans talk things over to arrive at a solution. Only humans see the world in subtle enough terms to realize that decisions needn't be all or nothing; some of what you want can be blended with some of what I want, and the result will be better for both of us.

Negotiation is such an essential human activity that a 110% approach to life necessarily includes a sensitivity to the nature of negotiation and the ability to make it work.

There is, of course, the structured, explicit negotiation – the situation in which Mr A and Ms B sit on opposite sides of a conference table and hammer out a contract, a labour settlement or a separation agreement.

Many other situations don't have that kind of formality, yet they are still negotiations. And they call for the same skills.

Say you are a teenager and you want to use the family car.

Your father wants the lawn mown. Your mother wants the basement cleaned. But meanwhile, it's Friday night, and Friday nights don't wait. You've got some negotiating to do.

Say you are a housewife and you've got workmen coming to paint your house. Their objective is to do the job as fast as possible and get their money. Your objective is not to have your home trashed in the process of being refurbished. You're going to be negotiating with the painters every step of the way. The bottom line is that negotiation is all around us. It's the way human beings get things done. You can't avoid negotiating, you can only be effective at it or ineffective at it.

The Elements of Persuasion

Negotiating is an *emotional* activity as well as a rational one. A negotiation takes on a momentum of its own. It becomes more than the sum of its parts – a little drama all by itself. The drama generates its own form of logic, one that is sometimes different from ordinary logic.

For that reason it is a fantasy to imagine that there is an airtight formula or set of rules that pertains to every negotiation. It simply doesn't work that way.

Still, there are two elements that should always be considered.

Timing

Children are uncanny at reading their parents' moods. And for all the talk about childish impatience, they're usually pretty good at waiting for the opportune moment before they ask for something.

This is a skill that adults forget. Maybe because we are taught that part of becoming a grown-up is to master our moods, to be rational, we like to think that we always judge every case strictly on its merits.

Well, that is a nice ideal to shoot for. But in actual practice, all of us are prey to a range of moods. We're more receptive at

181

some times than at others. For that reason, the success of a negotiation depends in no small part on simply when the negotiation happens.

If you want to use the family car, you don't ask Dad the minute he's inside the door, grumbling about what a lousy day he had and how his head is pounding. You wait until he's had a cocktail, smoked a pipe and smiled as you told him about the A you got on your maths test. Then you ask him, and away you go.

This same common-sense approach to timing pertains to negotiations where millions are at stake.

Tone

In the typical negotiation, one party wants something, the other party wants something else, and there is at least some component of conflict between the two. The existence of this conflict is not, in itself, a problem. That, after all, is why there is a negotiation in the first place.

What can become a problem is the hostile or uncooperative tone that results.

Let's come back to the lady and the housepainters. Her first priority is a neat job.

Clearly, there's an element of conflict; it takes time to lay drop-cloths, tape mouldings and so forth. Now, if the housewife begins this 'negotiation' by wagging her finger at the painters, browbeating them, telling them she'll sue if they get so much as one drop of paint on her carpets, that's setting a hostile tone. The chances are that the painters will respond by agreeing to everything she says – then doing precisely what they want as soon as she turns her back.

Why shouldn't they? No human bond has been formed. There has been no show of mutual concern or basic consideration. She's making the paint job an ordeal and a battle. The painters will probably respond in kind.

If, on the other hand, the lady begins by offering the painters a cup of coffee and Danish pastry, an entirely different tone is established. She can show them, by sitting them down in her spotless kitchen, how important her home is to her, how much pride she takes in it. She can admit to them that she's nervous about the disruption and possible mess. She can win their sympathy and make them want to do a neat job, even at the cost of a few extra hours.

In business situations, the importance of the tone of a negotiation can hardly be overstressed. It makes all the difference between a deal where the two parties truly feel like partners, and one in which people remain mistrustful and uneasy, always looking over their shoulder to see who's getting the best of it.

The Beauty of Yes

We have all known people who seem to take a diabolical delight in saying No. But in the great majority of situations, people would rather say Yes – because Yes is a beautiful thing.

Yes makes people feel good. It creates goodwill. Yes gratifies people. It makes them feel important that they are able to say Yes. It creates the warm glow of a good deed done and the satisfaction of being owed a favour.

I see negotiation as the process of clearing away the obstacles so that the other party can say Yes. The difference is subtle but crucial.

The Power of No

No is a mighty word. Around the age of two a child comes to understand that No is the way to establish his individuality. He can refuse to do things and hold out to get his way. The discovery of the concept of No is one of the pivotal moments in the life of every human being.

If one is uncertain, mistrustful or afraid, one can just invoke the negative and nothing will be lost – except, of course, an opportunity.

No is a shield. A good negotiator allows those on the other

side to feel comfortable enough so that the shield can be laid down and the real talking can begin.

There are many ways of persuading people to drop their armour, and maybe the easiest is simply to allow them the opportunity to get the No's off their chest. People like to make a strong gesture; they need to establish that they can't be pushed around. Once they've made that point, they become a great deal easier to deal with.

Let me illustrate this with a story from my early days with Arnold Palmer.

Arnold would go off on an exhausting round of tournaments and exhibitions, while I would stay behind in Cleveland. In actual fact, I was working as hard as Arnold was to promote his interests. But seeing it from Arnold's perspective, I was taking it relatively easy. I had the comforts of home, he was dragging himself from hotel to hotel. I had the relative calm of a daily routine, he had the pressures of competition.

Anyway, by the time Arnold returned, he'd be tired and needing to blow off steam. The 'steam' would take the form of saying No to the first few things I asked him to do. It didn't matter what my requests were. I think it's not unfair to say Arnold wasn't even listening to the requests. He simply had to go through the process of saying No.

The first couple of times this happened, I was unprepared and I made some mistakes. I asked Arnold something important while he was still in his No phase – and sure enough, he said No. He lost himself a fair bit of money that way!

Over time, I got to recognize the pattern and learned how to deal with it. I'd keep a number of unimportant things on hand, and I'd toss them into the air so that Arnold could take target practice.

This would go on for a while, and then I'd begin to see a change. Arnold's face would soften. His voice would become less insistent. He was getting to the end of his string of negatives and starting to feel sorry for me. You could almost see him thinking, 'Gee, I'm really unloading on McCormack, and the guy is only trying to do his job.' So then Arnold would be ready to approach a given question on its merits, and that's when I'd bring up the important points.

As Arnold and I got to know each other better and our friendship deepened, this dynamic almost got to be a joke with us. Sometimes I'd say to him, 'Arnold, are you ready for a serious question yet, or do you want to shoot me down a few more times first?'

The Golden Rule of Negotiating

It is obvious that, upon entering a negotiation, you should have a pretty clear idea, though a flexible one, of what you want.

Less obvious, but every bit as important, is the need to form a clear understanding of what the other side wants, and how, if at all, you can give it to them.

If you keep the emphasis on what you want, you are creating a situation where the other side can say No, we can't do that for you. If, on the other hand, you shift the focus to what they want, then you have the option of saying Yes or No, telling them you can go this far but not that far, you can make this work but you can't make that work.

Paradoxically, you have greater leverage when the other side is stating their case than when you are stating yours. You create more goodwill by trying to expedite the things they want to accomplish. You foster a tone of cooperation by trying to reconcile their needs with your needs. You gain information as you draw them out, and what they tell you will almost certainly be useful.

Is *cost* the first concern they mention? If so, then you're likely to meet resistance on matters of price and you've got to look for your own advantage elsewhere. If, on the other hand, their first aim is prestige or exposure, then the chances are that your benefit will lie in the monetary aspect of the deal.

The idea is to head off disagreements by finding out what is important to them, giving it to them if humanly possible, and taking your piece of the action from an area that is less important to them. That is profitable cooperation.

I will sometimes open a negotiation by simply saying, 'Tell me what you want.'

Spotting the Other Guy's Negotiating Tactics – and Stopping Him in His Tracks

If we have prepared well, we can transform the negotiating process into a pleasant dialogue that moves forward rationally and logically to a mutually desired conclusion.

Unfortunately, the other side doesn't always follow our script. If we are selling, the other side may not share our high opinion of our product or services. It may have policies against completing the sale. It may not have the money. All of these can be stumbling blocks in a negotiation.

But after years of bargaining, I've noticed that the same stumbling blocks keep appearing. In fact, certain arguments come up with such numbing regularity that I no longer regard them as arguments. I see them for what they really are. They are tactics designed to weaken my position but not to the point where I walk away from the table. They are not accurate indicators of what the other side thinks of me or my position. They are simply intended to elicit a response.

Negotiating tactics are like moves in a chess game. You don't overreact or get angry when someone makes a daring move in chess. At a certain level of play, you're expected to be familiar with the move, and you're expected to stay at the table and respond. The same thing happens in negotiations.

Here is how to handle some of the tactics you can expect from the other side of the negotiating table:

1. Don't accept the negative attack

Some people are bullies. You walk into their office and they pummel you with disparaging remarks about your company or your product. This is the crudest negotiating tactic of all. But some people have elevated it to an art form. They can turn the brutal invective on and off like a tap.

I know one executive who is probably not even aware that he does this. Whenever I meet with him to discuss a new project, he feels compelled to bring up a past project and home in on the one or two details out of a hundred that we performed less than perfectly. His tirades are so predictable they are comically easy to counter. For years now, the moment I greet him, I make a point of bringing up our alleged errors *first*. In that way I disarm him, taking away his primary weapon.

Some people – particularly young or inexperienced negotiators – fall for the negative attack.

Perhaps they are intimidated by the assault. (That is what the attacker wants. It is best not to react at all.)

Perhaps they feel guilty or responsible. (They should not. Remember, a bully doesn't need a valid reason to attack; it is in his nature to pick on someone who won't fight back.) Perhaps they believe that anyone venting that much fury must have a legitimate gripe. (Again, the attack is a tactic designed to break down your position. It is not personal. And it probably isn't valid.)

2. Don't accept their ultimatum

When people want to suggest that they are prepared to back out of a negotiation, they usually turn to a familiar set of phrases, such as 'That's all I can afford', or 'You have to do better than that', or 'Take it or leave it'.

These phrases work. They sound like ultimatums. They can scare the inexperienced negotiator into conceding anything in order to keep the buyer at the table and save the deal. But in reality, they are tactics. They are a test, another chess move to prod you into action, to see how well you counterpunch.

Ultimatums are rarely the end of a negotiation. They are often the beginning.

187

3. Don't give the buyer an easy way out

The easiest way out from any negotiation is 'I love your concept. I want to do it. But I don't have the budget.'

Oddly enough, this is different from 'That's all I can afford' because the first answer is not a tactic. When buyers tell you this, they aren't posturing; they really mean it. They don't have the budget. This provides an opportunity for you to ease into a negotiation at a price the buyer can't refuse.

For example, in our business of selling sponsorships to sports events, we are frequently told 'I don't have the money'. That is not surprising. Sports sponsorship is a fairly new sort of media buy and the price of entry is high.

But after months of identifying, pursuing and wooing a prospect who admits to loving our concept, we would be fools to let him leave the table. Sometimes we decide to work for nothing. We give the property away and let the customer pay whatever he thinks it is worth afterwards.

At other times we defer payment. This is like buying a car and paying for it later. But in our case it's much better than that. Our people rub shoulders with the customer's people for a year. He sees how we operate. If we do our job well, he'll not only pay us what he owes but go out of his way to find the budget for us in Year Two and beyond.

When someone tells you his budget is zero, your best response may be 'I can work with that'.

4. Beware the bulk order

Buyers are always looking for volume discounts – without actually buying the designated volume. If they secretly want 1000 units of your product, they'll try to get you to quote a price for 10,000 or 50,000 units and then start negotiating at the lower unit price. That is a fairly transparent tactic, requiring nothing more from you than the resolve to stick to your rate card.

But a clever negotiator can lure you into a discount in much more subtle ways. Real estate developers, for example, are masters at winning concessions from contractors by holding out the promise that there will be more work on other projects.

We've run into customers who insist on removing certain features from our proposal in order to lower the price, then having secured that price, try to negotiate those features back into the deal.

Some customers like to offer technical support, usually in the form of personnel, to lower the price, and then they never deliver their people.

There is some good news here, though. After all, when someone asks 'What if I buy two?', with a little patience and luck you may actually double your sales target.

5. Don't fall for the good cop

The good cop–bad cop tactic is one of the most familiar routines in negotiation. We've all seen it. Two people show up at the negotiating table. One of them is the designated bad guy, whose job is to chew you up, wear you down, make outrageous demands and challenge you every step of the way. The second person is the good guy, usually a senior person whose job is to apologize for his colleague's bad manners. Of course, you gravitate towards the good guy – because his temperament, demeanour and negotiating position appear to be more inviting.

The funny thing about the good cop–bad cop tactic is that I am very good at detecting it – but I fall for it anyway. In my heart I want to believe the good cop is on my side even when my brain is telling me that he is playing a role and his act is not necessarily in my best interest. I suppose this is a reflex from childhood: when we didn't get our way with one parent, we instinctively turned to the other. What we didn't know was that most parents have a tacit agreement never to contradict each other in front of their children.

How do you overcome good cop–bad cop? Simple. Shut out the good guy. Focus all your energies on turning the bad guy around to your point of view. If you can't do that, you haven't lost anything. You weren't going to do better with his partner anyway.

The 110% Concession

All negotiations have one thing in common: at some point, you will be expected to make a concession.

There is nothing wrong with that. Negotiation is, after all, give and take. Giving in is part of the drill.

Unfortunately, some people have a problem with this. They regard any concession as an admission of weakness or failure. I have seen negotiations fall apart even before they started because neither side was willing to concede on who would attend or on the venue.

I tend to go to the other extreme. I equate concession with winning. I never go into a negotiation without knowing exactly how much I am willing to concede.

Conceding a negotiating point is a golden opportunity to get something greater in return.

There are three ways to concede a point:

The 50% solution is to concede but get nothing in return

You would be amazed at how many people negotiate this way – because it is so easy to do. If the contractor renovating your house asks for a thirty-day extension, do you let him off the hook? Or do you ask for financial compensation or some other penalty in return?

Most people, I suspect, would let him off the hook. They want the contractor happy, not embittered, when he is working in their home and they want him to finish the job. They have the feeling that he is holding a gun to their head. What choice do they have if he can't finish on time? So they accommodate; it is the path of least resistance. You've made the other side happy. But other than goodwill, what have you got to show for it?

190

The 75% solution is to concede, but only for something of equal value

This is the tit-for-tat school of negotiating.

You want better payment terms? Place a bigger order.

You want a reduced price? Make a commitment today.

You want free shipping? Take delivery on Thursday.

You give an inch, you take an inch. The trouble is, you're never ahead of the game. Your position improves only as the other side's position improves.

The 110% solution is to concede but get more in return

This is the right approach, especially if the other side doesn't know how little the concession costs you.

People equate the value of a concession with how hard they work for it. If it takes them weeks of scrappy bargaining to win a price break from you, that concession somehow looms larger and more valuable than if you had given in on the spot. The net cost to you is the same, but the return can be far greater if you make the other side squirm. If you are alert, you can turn almost any negotiating point into a 110% concession.

A few years ago the chairman of a European conglomerate was dissatisfied with the size of his company's hospitality tent at a major sporting event. He wanted a larger tent and, since tents were limited, asked me if I could help.

I told him that I would try but explained that this would not be easy to orchestrate; in return, I expected some help on a television project being negotiated between our two companies.

It turned out that it was not difficult to secure the larger tent. The event directors thought that the smaller tent was a fire hazard and yielded quickly to my request.

But I didn't tell the chairman that. I waited a few weeks until the arrangements were locked in to bring him the good news. The chairman believed I had made a major effort on his behalf, and he was remarkably conciliatory in the television negotiation.

191

There is nothing particularly sly about this. As a negotiator, you are under no obligation to tell the other side that a concession is easy to make or immaterial to you. And you don't have to concede immediately.

In fact, conceding too quickly can paint you in a more unfavourable light than being difficult or intractable. I would be suspicious of someone who asks $100,000 for his product or service, and when I counter with a lowball offer of $50,000 accepts it on the spot (or agrees to split the difference). While I might be glad that I got my price, I would always be wondering what other points in the deal were similarly inflated.

Hardball

Every now and then you run across someone who looks you in the eye and lies to you. You deal with someone who signs a contract and then uses every technicality and legal dodge to avoid living up to its spirit.

In those situations, the negotiating techniques we've been talking about don't apply. Those techniques call for mutual respect, and if that context doesn't exist a different strategy is called for.

That is hardball, and it is not a pretty thing.

Hardball is a last resort, and playing hardball is qualitatively different from being a tough negotiator.

If you are operating honestly and in good faith, then even the most knock-down battle need not be damaging to a relationship. At the end of the day, people will shake hands, dust themselves off and go out and have a beer. Maybe people have got mad at each other. Maybe they have been exasperated. But the basic trust and respect are still intact. In some ways, the relationship has even been strengthened because you have learned to respect your opponent. No one has done anything unforgivable.

Hardball operates on the other side of that line.

Hardball is war. Don't play it any more often than you abso-

lutely have to. Don't play it unless you're ready to end a relationship. Don't play it unless you're damn sure you can win.

Let me give a brief example of a situation where a hardball strategy is called for.

Our company was approached by an individual who wanted to launch an athlete-management company in a country where we did not operate. This man was quite bright but very green. If he was going to succeed, he badly needed our expertise and an entrée to many of our connections around the world.

After a difficult but cordial negotiation, we prepared a contract that called for this man to pay us certain fees and commissions, pegged to the growth of his company, in exchange for the services we would render.

The problem, however, was that since our services were basically educational, we'd been rendering them all along. Every time we talked to this fellow, we were rendering service. We did so in good faith and on the assumption that he would sign the contract we had now agreed.

Since this fellow was operating in a foreign country, however, there were excuses for prolonging the contract-signing process. There were all sorts of technical questions of venue, jurisdiction and so forth. Still, we weren't worried; these things always take time.

Gradually, it dawned on us that this man never intended to sign the contract. He'd already got the bulk of the benefit without signing. As the months wore on, he needed us less and less. It became abundantly clear, to use the vernacular, that he was going to screw us.

Fortunately, we had one more card to play. Months before, I had agreed to speak at a seminar that was essentially the grand-opening event of his company. Many of the people he hoped to do business with would be there, as would the media. If this event fizzled, he would be off to a decidedly embarrassing start. And if I failed to appear, this fellow, at the very least, would have a fair amount of explaining to do.

I waited until seventy-two hours before the seminar, and then

I told him that if the contract wasn't signed by the time I reached the podium, there would be no speech.

This is the sort of ultimatum one should never use except in a hardball situation. It closes a door rather than opens one. It's like a medicine so powerful that it cures the disease but kills the patient.

In any case, the entrepreneur was stuck. He clearly couldn't reschedule the meeting, and his chances of finding another suitable speaker on three days' notice were virtually nil. I had him. He signed the contract. Do I like doing that sort of thing? No, I hate it. Am I proud of winning the war? Only to the extent that losing, when you know you're in the right, rankles.

Bartering Is Good Business

For most people, in or out of the workplace, barter is the abandoned child in the negotiating family.

Barter, they believe, is what you have to do when you can't afford to pay cash.

Barter is a sign of desperation.

Barter smacks of 'horsetrading'.

It doesn't feel legal or binding.

In fact, barter is more common than we think. Most of us make dozens of transactions every day that do not involve cash. We do this whenever we give of our time, our ideas, our goodwill, our expertise or our contacts.

Ordinarily, these transactions fall under the heading of favours. We do something nice for someone and *maybe* they will do something nice for us in return. But, we do not necessarily expect a *quid pro quo*.

Barter, however, is not a favour. Where the benefits of doing someone a favour are vague, the benefits of barter are explicit. Both sides know exactly what they are getting.

We barter all the time at IMG. If we are conducting a large volume of business in a certain city and know that we will continue to need hotel rooms there, we will approach a hotel

194

about an arrangement. In exchange for a fixed number of rooms at a special corporate rate, we will give the hotel free advertising at one of our events – perhaps a page in the tournament pro-gramme, a mention on the television broadcast or banners around the tennis court. We propose similar arrangements with airlines, rental car companies, limousine services, couriers and restaurants.

Our athletes barter their time and personal services for airline tickets, vacations, cars, office equipment, cases of rare wine, you name it.

One of the hidden attractions of barter is that it can turn a tough sell into an easy one. Say that we have established $25,000 as the price for a one-day personal appearance by a golfer. Also, let's say that the golfer needs a $25,000 security system for his home.

What if we approached the manufacturers of that security system and tried to interest them in paying $25,000 – in cash – for a one-day clinic conducted by our golfer for their top customers? Unless a decision-maker at that company was a rabid golf fan, that would be a tough sell.

Yet if we offered that one-day clinic *in exchange* for the company's $25,000 security system, the executives would be more likely to jump at it. Even with a conservative mark-up, their system probably costs them no more than $12,500 – so they are getting a clinic at 'half price'. Better yet, they are not spending cash. And our client gets what he wants without having to write a cheque. He has also found profit-able employment for a day that might otherwise have gone idle.

I realize that the average citizen doesn't have precious tele-vision time to give away, nor does he fix his 'day rate' at $25,000. But that shouldn't stop you from getting the most out of the transactions in your life. Assuming you have an intense aversion to spending cash, you need:

- a unique talent or product
- a heightened sense of people's desires

195

- a realistic sense of your worth

Let's take a closer look at these.

A unique talent or product

Actually, it doesn't have to be all that unique. Almost anything, from a professional skill to a hobby, can be bartered.

If I were an accountant, heavily reliant on computers, I might offer to do tax work for my computer supplier in exchange for hardware and maintenance.

I see no reason why doctors, lawyers or insurance salesmen couldn't barter their services in similar ways with their various suppliers. Or why the suppliers wouldn't welcome the arrangement. Each party should be overjoyed at avoiding the other's inflated mark-up.

You don't need an established skill or reputation to be able to trade on it. In fact, barter is a great way to get your foot in the door when you're starting out.

For one month, make a list of every one of your skills, in and out of the workplace. It can be anything from organizing a charity event to delivering a speech, from writing a successful proposal to repairing your car or coaching your child's soccer team. Then ask yourself, 'Who among my acquaintances could benefit from any of these talents?' You may be richer than you think.

A heightened sense of people's needs

Coming up with the cash is usually the stumbling block in most transactions. For some reason people want things they can't afford. So figure out what people *need*. Your ability to deliver that is limited only by your intelligence and imagination.

Many people never think about leveraging their expertise outside their profession.

I once had lunch with a professional copywriter at his favourite restaurant. The owner came by and handed the writer a press release announcing the opening of a new establishment. The two of us chuckled over the clumsy way the release was written.

There was an opportunity here for the writer, though I doubt he noticed it. A lot of people would let the moment pass, seeing no percentage in offending the restaurateur or wounding his pride.

But what if the copywriter told the restaurateur who he was and tactfully pointed out that the man was doing himself a disservice by sending out sloppy releases? What if he then offered to write all his press materials in exchange for $1000 worth of meals every quarter? I have a hunch that that kind of offer would be received positively by most restaurateurs. In fact, it would work at any public facility – a fitness centre, a tennis club, a country inn – that needed the occasional services of a good copywriter.

Over a three-month period, study your cheque-book and review your sales receipts and credit card statements. Pay attention to regular expenditures. You may be a more valuable customer than you think. Then ask yourself, 'If I had no cash, how would I have paid for these charges?'

A realistic sense of your worth

For many people, removing the cash element from a transaction removes their one true barometer of value. Since they are not spending money, they believe they are getting something for free. And when you dangle the word 'free' in front of people, they often lose their perspective. They begin to underestimate, rather than overestimate, the value of their time or talent.

We once represented a professional football player who had looked to us to leverage his celebrity into income outside of the National Football League. One of the income bases we established for this player was speaking engagements.

The executive assigned to the athlete had negotiated a princely $3500 fee (this was in the 1970s) for a speech in Detroit. It required the player to fly from his hometown, Chicago, spend the night in Detroit and speak at 9.30 a.m. the next morning. If

197

all went well, the player would be back home in Chicago for lunch.

The player said no, claiming he had better things to do than fly to Detroit.

A week later the player phoned our executive on another matter. There was a lot of noise in the background.

'Where are you?' asked the executive.

'I'm in an appliance store,' the player replied. 'The owner said he would give my wife a free refrigerator if I come in and sign autographs for the next six Tuesdays.'

Our executive was speechless. He didn't bother to explain that the refrigerator wasn't 'free' nor that the player could have bought ten refrigerators with the $3500 from the Detroit speech and had his next six Tuesdays to himself.

When people see the word 'free' they often abandon common sense and forget their true economic priorities. Barter often makes a greater impression than cash.

See It, Touch It, Talk to It

I know the business manager of a ballet company who persuaded a dentist to provide free dental care for the company's dancers in exchange for two subscriptions to the company's performances.

At first glance, this looked like a brilliant and one-sided deal for the ballet company – brilliant because American dance companies are notoriously strapped for funds and health costs always go up, one-sided because the tickets' face value was a fraction of the dental costs.

But don't tell that to the dentist. He won big, too. He received choice seats to the ballet, a prize normally reserved for patrons with deep pockets. Then there was the psychic compensation of helping dancers he admired. But the key element in the deal was the tangible, personal contact with the dancers. He got to know them and they in turn became acquainted with him and his work. It wasn't long before the dancers' referrals of new patients more than made up for the free care.

198

Perhaps the best thing about barter is that it can turn a routine transaction into something special.

One of our New York executives, a classical music *aficionado* and record collector, pays his Italian barber with tapes of rare opera recordings from his collection. The two of them discuss the next recording before each visit, and then they listen to it during the haircut.

This has been going on for more than ten years. The cost to both is nil – a blank tape and an otherwise empty barber chair. But you don't measure these arrangements purely in money saved or earned. Our executive has become the barber's favourite customer, someone he greets enthusiastically – and you can be sure it has nothing to do with the cut of his hair.

199

Epilogue

Since my early forties, when my children were still in grade school, people have asked me what I would do when I retired.

I responded then, as I do today, 'Why should I retire? Most people retire to something they have wanted to do all their lives. I am already doing it.'

I think what prompted the question was their curiosity about how long I could keep up the demonic pace I had set for myself at the time. Back then, I wanted all the 'mores' – *more* clients, *more* deals, *more* growth, *more* status, *more* success.

It must have appeared to friends and associates that I was racing towards a clearly marked finishing line, a finite goal – that attaining a certain number of clients or standard of living or measure of prestige would make me comfortable. That would be a reason to slow down, to demand less of myself.

What they couldn't see, of course, was the emotion that I brought to my effort. I really loved what I was doing. I still do. If they had felt what I was feeling, they would have been racing right alongside me, perhaps even faster.

I began this book with some heady notions about how to achieve superlative performance in business and in life. But there is one quality that I have intentionally left out, because it would be presumptuous of me to advise you on it.

The missing ingredient is *emotion*. You have to supply that on your own.

Let me give you an example of what I mean.

In 1955, Arnold Palmer had spent his first six months on the professional golf circuit, with very little success. He was very discouraged, and had actually considered quitting, when he came across a book that had been at the top of the best-seller lists ever since its publication several years before. The book was *The Power of Positive Thinking* by Norman Vincent Peale.

A few weeks later Arnold won the Canadian Open – his first professional tournament victory. He was playing *inspired* golf, and part of what enabled him to do so may have been this passage from Dr Peale's book:

I once played golf with a man who was not only an excellent golfer but a philosopher as well. As we went around the course the game drew out of him certain gems of wisdom, one for which I shall ever be grateful.

I hit a ball into the rough, into some high grass. When we came up to my ball I said, 'Now just look at that. I have a bad lie. It is going to be tough getting out of here.'

My friend grinned and said, 'Didn't I read something about positive thinking in your books?'

Sheepishly I acknowledged that was the case.

'I wouldn't think negatively about that lie of yours,' he said. 'Do you think you could get a good hit if this ball were lying out on the fairway on the short grass?'

I said I thought so.

'Well,' he continued, 'why do you think you could do better out there than here?'

'Because,' I replied, 'the grass is cut short on the fairway and the ball can get away better.'

Then he did a curious thing. 'Let's get down on our hands and knees,' he suggested, 'and examine the situation. Let's see just how this ball does lie.'

So we got down on our hands and knees, and he said, 'Observe that the relative height of the ball here is about the same as it would be on the fairway, the only difference being that you have about five or six inches of grass above the ball.'

Then he did an even more whimsical thing. 'Notice the quality and character of this grass,' he said. He pulled off a blade and handed it to me. 'Chew it,' he said.

I chewed, and he asked, 'Isn't that tender?'

'Why, yes,' I replied, 'It certainly does seem to be.'

'Well,' he continued, 'an easy swing of your number five iron will cut through that grass almost like a knife.' And then he gave me this sentence which I am going to remember as long as I live, and I hope you will also.

'The rough is only mental.'

To this day I remember the thrill, the sense of power and delight I had in the clean shot that dropped the ball to the edge of the green.

The rough is only mental: you can have all the talent and all the opportunities in the world – but if you love what you do, you will have found the 110% solution to life.